Small, tasty dishes
for moms
on the verge of a nervous breakdown

© 2007 Rebo International
This edition: © 2007 Rebo Productions b.v., Lisse

www.rebo-publishers.com
info@rebo-publishers.com

Text: Stéphanie de Turckheim and Aimée Langrée
Photography: Raphaële Vidaling
Design: Claire Guigal
Original title: Petits plats gourmands pour mamans au bord de la crise de nerfs
© 2006 Copyright SA, 12, Villa de Loucine, 75014, Paris, France
Translation: Barbara Beckers, Studio Imago
Editing: Studio Imago, Amersfoort

ISBN: 978-90-366-2169-4

Small, tasty dishes
for moms
on the verge of a nervous breakdown

50 stress-free recipes
that really go down
well with children

Text: Aimée Langrée and Stéphanie de Turckheim
Photography: Raphaële Vidaling

 REBO
PRODUCTIONS

Contents

Introduction 9

Get the children to eat. And what's more, if there are affinities… 16

Poetry 18

The Zen mom's ten keys 20

Anatomy of a mom 22

The RGIs: the Really Great Ideas 24

The plus and minus columns 28

The games page (to play with them) 30

Wednesday cooking class 32

Cooking workshop advice 36

Birthday advice 37

Tricks to get them to try everything 38

Vegetables and cereals

Children's words: My mom, she's the most brilliant mom… 42

· Clafoutis with crunchy vegetables 44

· Crumble with polenta and ratatouille confit 46

· Salad of carrot, beet, and apple spaghettis 48

· Pretty broccoli cake 50

· Tomatoes stuffed with bulgur wheat, risi bisi style 52

· Potato puree mashed with a fork 54

· Potato pancakes 56
· Our potato gratin 58
· Double treat: wholewheat spaghetti and vegetable spaghettis 60
· Spätzles 62
· Risotto with lemon and Gorgonzola 64
· Quick French fries 66

Meat and small complete dishes

Moms' words: random thoughts and maxims 70
· Shepherd's pie with vegetables 72
· Baked ramekins 74
· Slice of bread topped with egg 76
· Browned breaded escalopes 78
· Mini cordon-bleu parcel 80
· Sticky chicken 82
· Children's sushis 84
· Tiny stew 86
· Pitta pizza 88
· Island fisherman casserole 90

Desserts

Moms' words. Did I really say that? Well, yes, actually.. 94
· Alsace apple tart 96
· Smooth chocolate dessert 98
· Succulent layers 100
· Mini-pancakes with cream cheese, vanilla sugar, and stewed fruits 102
· Au pair's cream cheese tart 104
· Tartlets and tarts 106
· Gateau moistened with fruits 108

· Banoffee pie   110
· Grated apples with rosemary honey and orange   112
· Grandma's crystallized apples and quick custard   114
· Gateau supreme with coconut   116
· Soft dessert with lemon   118
· Mom's iced strawberry gateau   120

Snacks, parties, and breakfasts

A little advice between friend   124
· Light cake with banana and white icing   126
· Welcome cake with orange blossom   128
· Chocolate cookies   130
· Quick flapjacks   132
· Mouthwatering crunchy crumble with cream   134
· Fruited bread slices   136
· Cooking workshop: "Christmas cookies"   138
· Cooking workshop: "Coconut mice"   140
· Small mouthfuls, balls, and croquettes   142
· Strawberry syrup Princess gateau   144
· Knights' gateau   146
· Magic cake   148
· Children's buffet   150
· Iced chocolate gateau balls   152

Everyone's asleep: the warrior's break   154
Recommended soundtrack   156
Ingredients' index   158
The genesis of the book   160

MOM : [momma] n. f. (1121 ; *momma,* 1584 ; children's formation by doubling the letter "m" ; Cf. gr. and lat. *Mamma*). ◊ **1°** Children, even in adulthood, use this affectionate term when referring to their mother. *! I'll call you, mom…,* song. *Mom's gone out, she's going to come back. Where's your mom? I don't know, my little one, ask mom.* ◊ **2°** *The mom,* the mother of the family. To play at being mom.

**adapted from
Petit Robert 2002**

Introduction

Riddle: "I'm in the kitchen three times a day, three hundred and sixty-five days a year. Who am I?" Clue: I'm sometimes greeted with a cheerful expression, sometimes with a big "grouch," and then someone says: "So what? It's cool, mom made it!"

Have you guessed? That's right, welcome to the moms' club!

The "mom" thing starts with the first "waa" at the hospital, and with the tiny breath that alights on your skin... Or perhaps with this dark blue and oh so serious gaze that you encounter right away... But it's strange how quickly these moments come when we go shopping with our hair mussed for the fiftieth time in the week and with great effort we work out all the next tasty and imaginative meals we're going to have to concoct, between the kids coming out of school, the next daft thing they get up to, and the last slobbery kiss of the day. There's no end to it... But despite everything, we really love this marathon of madness. Wooden cross, Iron Cross... Our hearts are full of love, the house is full of shouting and finger marks. Don't panic! Get to work!

We've been collecting recipe books since our earliest childhood, passionate about our food as we are. But trying to get our children to eat, teach them the taste of life, awaken their senses, convey the idea of health to them, and arouse their gustatory curiosity is a different ball game!

We started by looking at how women friends were doing, and then observed the reactions of children, and we even organized cooking classes and workshops on Wednesday afternoons. And next, we wanted to gather together the fruits of these observations in a book—a book that is a compilation of all our little secrets, respectable and shameful.

This book is going to do you good if, like us, you find yourself humming Fugain's song sometimes...

Even while running, faster than the wind, faster than time...
Even while flying,
I won't have the time, the time
To visit the immensity of such a vast universe...
Even in a hundred years,
I won't have the time, the time.

Take the time (just a little will be enough). It's worth it. A weakness for good food is a great virtue. This book is aimed at every mom with children, at every child with a mom. It has the genuine feel of recipes that have been passed between women friends, after supper or a birthday tea, when surrounded by cheerful faces and empty plates.

Here's our five-point creed:
1. No nonsense! Recipes that really work.
2. They'll try everything before the age of 6.
3. The truth about children! Don't live in a dream world in which well-behaved cherubs will spend three hours making a flaky pastry and a chocolate and raspberry cream filling.
4. Cooking is precise, simple, recreational, sensual, manual labor.
5. Cooking is pure love.

We've tested, started from scratch again, and tried every recipe with our little angels over a period of one year in cooking class, until they're perfect, irreproachable, and simple to make. As we were once little girls ourselves, we have our own sweet and sugary memories: and this is the realization of a gustatory regression. Objects, textures, tastes—we needed to rediscover them. Like the great thrill

of a little vanilla cream that is just warm. And like the aromas of a countryside Christmas workshop…

And yet, one conclusion can be drawn: children aren't nostalgic about their childhood. Well, it's hardly surprising, they're in the midst of it!

What they need is to discover new things, overcome their problems with trying something different, and be proud of saying: "I made that!" It's all about weighing, kneading, chewing, tasting, hating, comparing, loving. Kids have something to say about everything, and believe us when we say that at their age, if they don't like something, they really don't like something!

It has to be good.
It has to look good.
Above all, it has to
be practical!

Goodbye to fuss,
and to gimmicks
that you grow tired
of too quickly, and to
impractical   recipes.
(Bear in mind that the
attention span of todd-
lers is 30 minutes if
you're lucky!) Goodbye
to dodgy chemicals and

colorings. Goodbye to meals that drag on, and boring or ridiculous menus. We've used basic, natural, and simple ingredients—butter, eggs, milk, sugar... The basics, but also a lot of fruit, green vegetables, and other fresh ingredients. We aimed at simplicity, speed, and variety. Nothing is too good for these little monsters, eh?

There was a great temptation for the children to produce nothing but sweet recipes. But in everyday life we eat

balanced meals. No sooner is one meal finished than moms have to come up with an idea for the next... In this book, you'll find recipes for every day of the week, ideas, and tips to transform meals into something enjoyable and successful. And then, there are the party recipes and Wednesday cooking workshops in which the children are the stars.

We haven't classified the recipes in order of service: "appetizer, main course, cheese, and dessert," because children are not so formal. A meal always takes too long for them, and they're happier with one that fits the stock phrase "a big plateful followed by a small plateful." Use a doll's tea set. Sometimes, it's great if everything is tailormade to their size. (It's also useful to recall the 1950s cult film The Incredible Shrinking Man, as you can then appreciate that our little kids live in a disproportionate world in

relation to their size.) A small table, place settings, minicheeses, minivegetables, small desserts, presented in small pots or dishes…They're very easily pleased.

All our recipes serve 4–5 people. OK, an average family, if some statistics are to be believed, consists of 1.8 children, but who's ever seen 1.8 children at the table? It's made even less likely because there's always a little friend to invite—or, what's more, an adult friend, because these children's recipes go down rather well with adults too!

In short, if there were only one cookbook that you could take to a desert island, this would be it. Well, if the book's in your kitchen instead, that's fine. To be honest, a desert island is not always practical…

MOM : from the Greek *mamma,* a disheveled person (although always very pretty) of the female sex, generally responsible for the domestic life and the home (*sic*). ◊ **1°** Person constantly deprived of sleep, who, after a fashion, tries to face up to a reality which is beyond her belief. ◊ **2°** Human being who juggles with a chicken pox epidemic, mending a cuddly bear's eye, the pursuit of a possible career, water damage because the Playmobile® is stuck in the toilet, cf. *Mom stays in Zen mode...* Her diary of canceled appointments, her lists and her lists of lists, her need for a good haircut, the loads of cuddles she gives, her permanently empty refrigerator, her existential questions about the life of the couple (e. g. : *I do everything here, or what ?*), the dog's rheumatism, and the babysitter's moods. Popular : *Mom only has two hands, hell !* ◊ **3°** Person satisfied with life.

Get the children to eat.
And what's more, if there are affinities...

Once upon a time, there was a world in which a portion of meat accompanied by vegetables and starch was considered to be the ideal meal for fast-growing children. And a world in which these same children, who were mega well behaved (it did happen) would sit down at table, delighted to have the same kind of meal every day, and every week too.

OK, it's a lovely myth, but does it still make children and moms dream about this world in full "gustatory transformation?" Nowadays, we talk of variety, balance, sensation... of pleasure, eh! Let's just admit that the problem isn't simple: we've had mad cows, fish fed in a bizarre way in polluted seas, dodgy milk, eggs, and cheeses—the classics of the thirty prosperous years between 1945 and 1975 that regularly give rise to new debates with regard to the relationship between nutrition and safety, and so on.

Um... So what are we left with, then? Our good sense. Our love, our humor, our energy. Already things don't look so bad.

In fact, it's a lot easier and nicer to feed children than is generally believed, even when

taking into account their incredible ability to reject, refuse, and scatter food about, when they're not using it as modeling clay or a ping-pong ball. It's normal for all children to pick at their food. Remember how you were at the age of 5. And onward and upward!

GOOD EATING HABITS START IN THE CRADLE

You're sure to be told that it starts well before that, but this is not our suggestion in this book... We believe wholeheartedly that food is very much more than fuel.

It's a simple, everyday craft. It's the most intimate language, the most emotional and sensual language between the child and the world. Not sure whether you can teach it? No, but you can encourage it.

If we want our children to enjoy their food, we have to give them tasty things. There should be no strict rules, no obsession, nor any feelings of guilt: our instinct dictates what is a fair balance between necessary (and adored) "junk food" and small homemade dishes. A love of good food must be as natural as breastmilk or as a ray of sunlight in summer. By developing her instinct, a mom is constructing the foundations of the building.

Ah! Yes! A final bit of advice, but not any less important: moms everywhere, from all regions, don't ever forget this: it's impossible to convey the message of the pleasure to be found in good food if you don't experience it yourselves. A mom who's into food, and is herself appealing and attractive too (who'll always have the time to go on a diet in another life), is the best foundation!

Be into food, and be reckless. Explain, share. Make sure you eat as well!

Poetry

My dear children,
I love you in the evening,

I love you in the morning,
On Tuesdays and the rest of the week too.

My love for you is greater than the Grand Canyon
More beautiful than a truck,

My greatest loves, my birds,
My love for you is sweeter than a horse's nostrils…

OH NO!
WHAT ARE THESE FELT-TIP PEN DRAWINGS DOING ON THE
LIVING-ROOM WALL?

The Zen mom's ten keys

1 — Get used to the idea that your children are going to like what's on offer, instead of fearing their (future) refusal. Surprise yourself, have faith in them.

2 — Offer small portions, which can be tried again. Nothing is more frightening to a child than a large overfilled plate.

3 — Give them "real" food. No child under the age of 6 needs low-fat products or food with added sweeteners. Serve dishes that you want to eat with them—really nice things that are both possible and recommended for sharing with other adults.

4 — Get them to join in. The more they help, the more they'll understand... Therefore, the more they'll like what they eat. And not just cakes and desserts. Everyday meals are the building blocks of life.

5 — Organize your shopping well. Buy fresh, ready-to-use basics: make sure they're always fresh. Go shopping with the children. (Oh.... a logistical nightmare, but in actual fact, it's good to let them admire what's on offer and choose what they'd like.)

6 – Make sure that you serve a bit of everything every day. Fruit, vegetables, dairy products... if it's fried or served with a little sauce, don't make a big thing out of it. As far as a healthy diet is concerned, it's what's lacking that makes the difference...

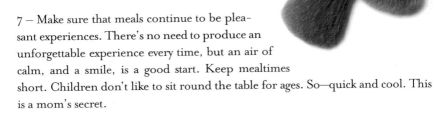

7 – Make sure that meals continue to be pleasant experiences. There's no need to produce an unforgettable experience every time, but an air of calm, and a smile, is a good start. Keep mealtimes short. Children don't like to sit round the table for ages. So—quick and cool. This is a mom's secret.

8 – Play with them, be crafty, spring surprises, negotiate... A compromise is enough: they'll try a mouthful out of respect but what they leave on the plate is too exhausting (for you!). Food fads, like what they leave on the plate, come and go of their own accord. Have patience.

9 – Don't ask them to make choices all the time. Would you like strawberry or cherry yogurt, my darling? It's too difficult for them. Mom has prepared it. There you go. End of story. Strawberry it is!

10 – Don't feel guilty if you don't provide three delicious, sophisticated, and healthy meals a day (it's been proved scientifically that this isn't within the realms of possibility). There's no such thing as perfect parents. And if Superman® and Lois Lane had small children, even they would soon realize their limits. So there you go!

Anatomy of a mom

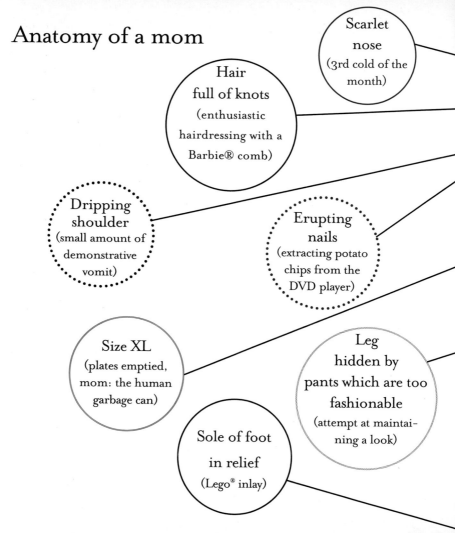

Scarlet nose (3rd cold of the month)

Hair full of knots (enthusiastic hairdressing with a Barbie® comb)

Dripping shoulder (small amount of demonstrative vomit)

Erupting nails (extracting potato chips from the DVD player)

Size XL (plates emptied, mom: the human garbage can)

Leg hidden by pants which are too fashionable (attempt at maintaining a look)

Sole of foot in relief (Lego® inlay)

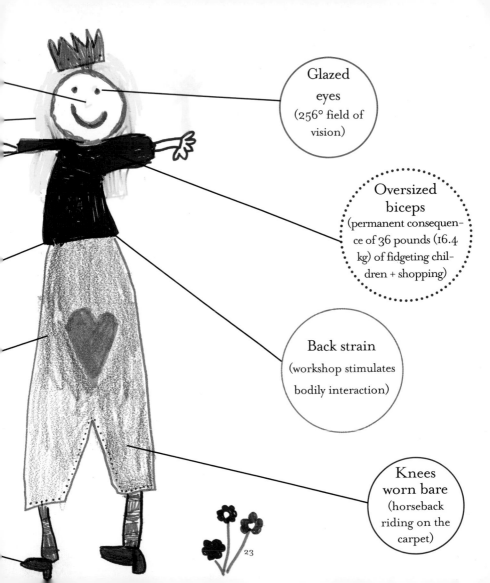

Glazed
eyes
(256° field of
vision)

Oversized
biceps
(permanent consequen-
ce of 36 pounds (16.4
kg) of fidgeting chil-
dren + shopping)

Back strain
(workshop stimulates
bodily interaction)

Knees
worn bare
(horseback
riding on the
carpet)

23

The RGIs : the Really Great Ideas

Clever products that quickly become indispensable when you've acquired a taste for them.

Basic shopping

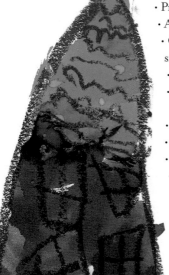

- Sandwich loaves from the baker
- Good dessert chocolate
- Precooked brown rice
- All kinds of pasta
- Organic bouillon (made in small cubes)
- Fine semolina
- Dried fruits instead of candies: mango, pineapple, bananas, apples…
- Green and pink lentils
- Homemade jelly
- Soy milk with calcium
- Tomato puree
- Mild mustard
- Sweetened condensed milk
- Liquid honey
- Extra virgin olive oil
- Italian breadsticks
- Compote in a tube
- Real vanilla pods
- Japanese soy sauce
- Roasted or ground almonds
- Spices, spices, and more spices…

Utensils

- Nonstick baking sheet (rectangular with a raised edge of approximately 1 cm)
- Nonstick molds + a round mold with hinge
- Various wooden spoons and plastic spatulas
- Dishes for children (unbreakable ones)
- Small china or cast iron dishes
- Pastry cutters of different shapes
- Small super-sharp cheese grater
- Small food processor or universal juicer
- Colored sealable containers
- Mandolin (Japanese grater)
- Pretty aprons for children
- Heart-shape mold
- Waxed paper
- Wok
- Oven mitt
- Round grid for pastry making
- Funny eggcups
- Steamer for cooking couscous
- A good whisk

The bottom of the refrigerator

- Really fresh milk
- Light cream
- Readymade flaky pastry
- Various grated cheeses (Swiss cheese, Cantal, Parmesan)
- Soft cheese—such as "The Laughing Cow" variety
- Cream cheese—40% fat
- Eggs bought from a market
- Salted farmer's butter
- Ham
- Stewed fruits
- Vacuum-packed cooked beets
- Deep-frozen basics (uncooked)
- Fresh lemons for seasoning
- Gervais cheese

Extras that come in handy

- Drawer of little surprise presents
- Vegetable preserves in glass jars
- Orange blossom water
- Crystallized lemons
- Olive puree
- Pure butter cookies
- Salt flour
- Colored sugars
- Organic instant custard flan mix
- Confectioner's sugar for decoration
- Small wooden toothpicks
- Almond puree, sesame puree
- Self-rising flour
- Organic corn syrup or British golden syrup
- British digestive biscuits (cookies)
- British lemon curd
- Chestnut puree
- coconut milk
- Pitta bread

And don't forget a little chilled white wine, for mom and dad…

The plus and minus columns

Rainy afternoons, 4 to 5pm, the horrendous rush hour, the shouting, the arguments, the ghastly class photos, the playgrounds on rainy days, the whims, the tantrums, the jealousies, the toys that overrun the house, the awful incidents with guests, the diapers, the animals they don't take care of, the Oedipus complex, the runny noses, the bad language, the stupid things they do, the spankings, the vaccines, the high temperatures, the provocations, the refusals, waking up in the night, the yelling, the never-ending bedtime ritual, the piano lessons…

Hang on in there!

Because firstly there are all of these, too:
The children's words that spill out, the snuggling in our necks, the tickles, the secrets, the declarations of love, the discoveries, the drawings, the friends of both sexes, the wish to do well, the dresses that swirl, the grazed knees, the first star on the ski slopes, the desire to grow up, the fear of the wolf that makes them quiver with joy, the end of year show, being asleep in our arms, the scent of their skin, the sticky kisses, the presents on Mother's Day, the little feet in adult shoes, the profound questions, the little mouse, the school poems, the catch-me-if- you-can games, the summer camp postcards, the playgrounds on sunny days, the reunions, the princess costumes, the superheroes aged 3, the exaggerations, the piano lessons…

And then there's them, them, them…

When you need a moment's peace...

Picture sudoku for kids

Dear Children,

Maybe you already know there are some great games that you can play without any help from Mom! Picture sudoko, for instance. It's a fun game for smart kids, you need to use your brains to play it, and you can draw in Mom's book without making her mad at you!

These sudoku puzzles are really simple — each one uses only four pictures.

Fruit'n'veg sudoku: carrot + tomato + pear + apple

Cook's sudoku: cook's hat + saucepan + cooking spoon + saltshaker

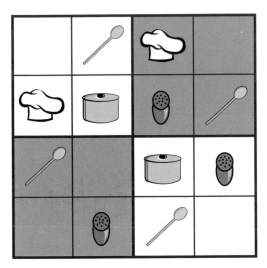

Put the right pictures on the empty shelves. But be careful! None of the pictures can be repeated in the same row, in the same column, or in the same square with four shelves. (And don't even think about mixing pictures from the fruit'n'veg sudoku with pictures from the cook's sudoku!) Let's go, get solving!

And now it's down to you to think up more quizzes, riddles, imaginative games, so that you give the children a message and let them join in: this will encourage them to be responsible.

Mommyyy!!!!! I've done it!!! Come play with me!

Wednesday cooking class

This is an account with photos of a day spent cooking with a small group of children. On the menu: Christmas cookies, chocolate mousse, and coconut mice—not to mention the improvisations…

Stéphanie is looking after the older children… and Aimée the younger ones. Félix is learning how to roll out pastry. Dahlia and Céleste are cutting it out with the pastry cutter. There's a crucial choice to be made and the girls are

debating: which shape do you prefer? It's a debate that sets Basile thinking. Pastry cutters don't do much for him: he prefers to mold with his fingers. Now Antoine has decided to

master a rolling pin that is almost bigger than he is. His dungarees look good, but I hope success doesn't depend on experience…

Hugo is a specialist: he makes twelve crescent moons all by himself. They're heavenly, and he adds the finishing touches with a brush: "They seem to be made of gold!" To complete this alchemic process, Stéphanie puts the treasures in the oven and takes them out again when they've just browned and are ready to eat. The aroma prises Edgar from his bedroom. What's the next course? The next course is a chocolate mousse. Stéphanie melts the chocolate under the strict supervision of the twins. She adds the eggs, separating the white from the yolk, while sticking out her

tongue so as not to crush the shells. Then comes the essential stage: trying it... and getting the others to try it!

As a privilege of his age, Hugo is in charge of the
whisk, the machine that produces a stiffly beaten
mixture... Victory: the mixture has set! The girls

show off their trophy (this is
normal: they're the ones
who held the bowl) and

Antoine tries it again, as a
mark of professionalism. They blend
the mixture and put it in the
refrigerator for the dessert...

and seven kids volunteer to do the
dishes with their fingers! The next
challenge: to make little mice out of a
coconut mix, and most importantly, numerous
edible accompaniments (candies, pastilles, small
licorice sticks, sugar marbles...). Stéphanie makes
a model. Everyone is free to draw inspiration

from it, or to create
an imaginary creature as they please.
She cuts the gelled candies in two to
suggest ears. Each child is engrossed in
producing a three-dimensional
masterpiece that doesn't even need to
be put in the oven before it's enjoyed;

letting it harden at room temperature is enough.

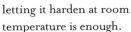

The licorice is changing into small red sticks. They keep an eye on their neighbor's mouse, which gives them ideas. And, in any case, why stick to ordinary white mice with only two eyes and just one tail? After half an hour of intense labor, a race of mutant mice gradually materializes… The workshop draws to a close: the twins choose from the photos.

Cooking workshop advice

· If you're by yourself, avoid groups of more than five children. Four is ideal.

 · Group the children together in age brackets: the 3–4-year-olds, the 5–6-year-olds… The older children will finish first and they'll be delighted to pass on their newly acquired knowledge to the younger children.

· Plan a session in two stages, and therefore make two dishes. While the first dish is cooking in the oven, they can work on the second.

· Essential: decoration. This aspect alone often takes longer than the rest of the entire recipe, and that's how it should be! As far as decoration is concerned, forget all your prejudices about "good taste" and let them express their creativity. Too bad if you can't even see the cake anymore under a mountain of candies!

· You can never say this too often: be careful of hot dishes straight from the oven. Try as you might to tell children this, they reach out with their hands all the same, particularly toward hot plates. One solution is to cook small cakes on waxed paper and to place this kind of paper on the table when you take them out of the oven. OK, it's hot, but their hands won't stick to it as they would to a metal plate…

· Always start by showing the end result by way of the model (e.g. for the coconut mice). Oral explanations are not enough.

· Consider providing the children with small utensils adapted to the size of their hands, even if it means making spatulas out of pieces of wood collected in the forest…

Birthday advice

• Several children busy playing together in someone else's house are often too excited to concentrate on food, even if it's party food. Make do with a dazzling cake and a few snacks; don't make too many (you'll feel disheartened).

• The children will be more bowled over by the decoration than by the recipe itself. Don't have any hangups about digging out a trusty old yogurt gateau recipe, provided you let your imagination run away with you as regards its external appearance.

• Be prepared to see your efforts and concerns vanish at the same time: birthday food is often gulped down in 4 minutes. And whoosh! The imps run off to play again at 60 miles an hour.

• Create a kind of party menu that will come in useful for several birthdays with a few variations on the presentation theme: children have no objection to repetition. In fact, the very opposite! And then, you've found a way of inventing a family tradition…

• Don't try to please other parents. The party is meant to be for your children!

• Don't panic about the quantities of sugar or colorings that they'll guzzle on their birthday. It's not the right moment to worry: you have the whole of the rest of the year for that…

Tricks to get them to try everything

• We like fresh herbs. But often, children announce that they don't like anything green. All of a sudden, the sight of herbs sprinkled over their plate horrifies them. The law of contradiction or simple curiosity will make them try them one day. Put the herbs in a small container on the table. Explain that they can help themselves to anything they like the look of. That way they won't moan. Each child can help themselves to more if they want. If they don't choose anything, that's just too bad. There will be all the more for you.

• Associate new things with ingredients they already like. Try cauliflower served with tomato sauce, parsnips rolled in ham, a compote of quinces that they can sprinkle themselves with vanilla sugar if they like…

• Always take trouble over the decoration: color contrasts, an entertaining plate, an edible spoon… Children are very responsive to this.

• A mom's trick: tell them stories while they're eating. First, it entertains them: they forget to say "no." And then, it makes them want to take an active part in the intrigue while opening their mouths. A few examples: the poor, sad beet that goes on a world tour in search of someone who'll agree to eat it, or the (very) large pea family that needs to be reunited at the bottom of their stomachs so that the family members are not separated…

• Arrange a few spices, a little sauce, lemon, and herbs on the table… Each child cooks up something to eat and there's an aroma of freedom that envelops the kitchen, making them want to try their own experiments. You'll know this has worked when the child stops refusing their omelet after disguising it with paprika!

Vegetables and cereals

Children's words

« My mom, she's the most brilliant mom… »

She plays jokes. When I was 5, she made a half-cake for my half-birthday.
Clara, aged 5

When she goes out, she's pretty and she smells nice.
Tom, aged 5

She uses swear-words. She thinks I don't notice them.
Nathaniel, aged 6

For
work my mom
gives classes to
computers and she
cooks my food.
Alexander, aged 4

My mother does
magic tricks with
matches. One day, she
burned herself, but she
hadn't hurt herself. She's
too strong!
Lottie, aged 8

My mom, she's
the most brilliant
of all. She always eats
black bananas. That way I
can always have new
ones.
Paul, aged 5

She
says she's going
to blow her top.
What's a top?
Zelda, aged 4

When I had chicken
pox, she washed my
forehead with a cold thingy,
then I went to sleep. When
I woke up, she was still there!
Juliette, aged 6

Clafoutis with crunchy vegetables

All moms are preoccupied with their failures, their theories, and their little spiel about vegetables. Have you forgotten? This is how it works: we'd say that vegetables are good, that we don't even mention them, and that we use them. Period. That's how it's always been and our children are no worse or better than other kids. (Well, just a tiny bit more wonderful, and we don't say that because they're ours!) In short, cherry clafoutis deserved to be hijacked. This is a complete small dish that we serve in individual minipots. Children adore it. Frozen vegetables are suitable for this recipe, because they stay crunchy.

· 3 eggs
· 3 tbsp liquid cream
· 1 tbsp all-purpose flour
· 1/2 cup milk
· 1 pinch nutmeg
· 3 tbsp grated cheese (Parmesan, Swiss cheese, or Comté)
· Generous 4 cups frozen vegetables: chopped tomatoes, zucchini, red and yellow peppers, peas, or tasty fava beans… on their own or mixed

Preheat the oven to 400 °F (200 °C). Beat the eggs with the cream in a bowl. Slowly add the all-purpose flour, the milk, the nutmeg, and then lastly the cheese. The mixture should be very smooth. Put the vegetables in an oven dish and pour the mixture into it, while gently blending, so that it's evenly distributed. Bake in the oven for 50 minutes to 1 hour.

One piece of advice about vegetables: don't take it personally if they refuse something, here or there. Aren't they entitled to dislike Brussels sprouts and fricasseed gourds?

Crumble with polenta and ratatouille confit

We no longer speak highly of the merits of crumbles. They're all famous—made with red fruits, apples, rhubarb… But they go well with savory ingredients, too. Children can roll up their sleeves and shuck the ingredients themselves. Crumble is an absolute favorite with them, it's a summer treat, a crumble is for midday. Make it distinctive.

- 2 lb (1 kg) ratatouille
- 1/2 stick butter, softened
- 2 tbsp all-purpose flour
- 2 tbsp polenta
- 2 tbsp grated Parmesan

Thoroughly cook the ratatouille, until you obtain a compote consistency or vegetable confit (children don't like lumps very much). Blend the butter, the all-purpose flour, the polenta, and the Parmesan with your fingertips. When you've obtained a granular mixture, arrange it over the ratatouille in an oven dish. Bake in a moderate oven (350 ° F / 180 ° C) for 35 minutes, until the crumble is golden brown.

NB: nowadays you can find very good deep-frozen ratatouille in the stores, which cooks easily. You can make it more palatable for children by adding whatever their preference is: tomato puree, olives, zucchini, herbs…

Salad of carrot, beet, and apple spaghettis

Raw or cooked, kids should really like these! Ah… vegetables! Our secret trick: grated vegetables, Japanese style. It's true that in the land of the Rising Sun, the art of long, crunchy grated vegetables has been perfected. The important thing for the Japanese is to be very careful with their fingers, because the blades they use are megasharp! With carrots, zucchini, apples, raw beets, black or pink radish, you obtain an excellent consistency that is firm and pretty. We've discovered that the key instrument can be found in most places and is called a mandolin. The Japanese version is found in stores that sell organic products. It's indispensable. You should use the intermediary grid for the best cut.

- I carrot
- I raw beet
- I sharp apple
- 1/2 cup grated Comté or Cheddar cheese
- 2 tbsp virgin olive oil
- A little sea salt
- Juice of I orange

Grate the carrot, the beet, and the apple lengthwise, to produce "spaghettis." The longer they are, the prettier they'll be (and funnier). Do the same with the Comté or Cheddar. These cheeses are often sold in rectangular shapes, and are therefore practical to grate lengthwise with the mandolin. For the vinaigrette, beat the oil, the sea salt and the orange juice (which you'll use instead of vinegar). Pour the vinaigrette onto the plate, over the vegetable spaghettis, without mixing them—so that you don't break them.

NB: when children's taste for raw vegetables develops, try the same salad with young, very firm zucchini. Wonderful!

Pretty broccoli cake

Each slice resembles a landscape, which children find magical. For your information, broccoli is packed with fiber, antioxidants, and vitamins. The salted cake, in slices or cubes, is ideal for a picnic at home. It makes a change from sandwiches. It should be firm (and not too sticky), so that it doesn't crumble. This recipe is a base for all other savory cakes.

- I good head (approx. I lb / 500 g) of very green broccoli
- 3 eggs at room temperature
- I 3/8 cups all-purpose flour
- 3 tbsp olive oil
- I cup milk at room temperature
- I pinch nutmeg
- I tsp baking powder
- 7 tbsp grated cheese
- Small salad (optional)
- Lemon mustard sauce (optional)
- Cherry tomatoes (optional)

Preheat the oven to 400 °F (200 °F). Boil the broccoli for 2 minutes, and strain it on a paper towel. Mix the eggs, all-purpose flour, oil, milk, nutmeg, baking power, and cheese in a bowl for 5 minutes. Fill a cake mold two-thirds full with the mixture, then plant broccoli flowerets like little trees, close together, in the center of the mold. Cover with the rest of the mixture. The children can play gardeners to help you. Bake in the oven for I hour until the inside is cooked. Gently turn the cake out of the mold while it's still hot. Serve warm or cold, we suggest with a small salad spiced up with a lemon-mustard sauce or with cherry tomatoes spiked with toothpicks.

Here's a trick to make sure that the vegetables are really green: add I pinch baking soda to boiling water. Try this with navy beans, peas... Other savory combinations that work well together are goat's cheese and olives, peas and bacon cubes, Roquefort and crushed filberts.

Tomatoes stuffed with bulgur wheat, risi bisi style

Risi bisi is a charming name behind which a simple spring recipe is hidden— Italian, of course: a small green and white risotto with fresh flavors. This is our interpretation of it, using a wholewheat cereal that is easy to digest. It's a nourishing little meal, and it's healthy and quick to make. It's easy for moms, and it's entertaining for children. They like finding green peas mixed with bulgur wheat or with a variety of cereals under the tomato hat. You need beautiful large tomatoes with soft pulp and firm skins. Don't be tempted to use tomatoes which are "in clusters"—they're primarily cultivated in greenhouses.

- 4 large tomatoes, if possible with stalks
- 1/2 cup precooked bulgur wheat
- 1 tbsp olive oil
- 2 tbsp peas
- A little ground salt and pepper
- Grated Parmesan
- Chopped aromatic herbs (optional)

Preheat the oven to 400 °F (200 °C). Cut the top off each tomato carefully, without removing the stalk or the green part, which you set aside to make a lid. Scoop out and crush the pulp in a bowl, then blend in the bulgur wheat. Add the oil, the peas, and a little salt and pepper. Bake in the oven for 15–20 minutes. Before serving, lift the "hat" and sprinkle some fresh Parmesan, and some chopped herbs if you wish, on top.

Potato puree mashed with a fork

You will already have the puree recipe that is "the real McCoy." You know that you need floury potatoes cooked just right, a genuine potato masher so as not to spoil the texture, a good quantity of slightly salted farmer's butter, and a little nutmeg... Yes, you know all that already. But what we like is puree mashed with a fork. You don't do anything (hardly) and the kids think you're great... You have supper early. You go to bed early. Everything's going well.

- 2 lb (1 kg) potatoes
- Butter
- 1 pinch nutmeg (optional)
- Top-quality salt

Steam the potatoes. We prefer new potatoes, including the skin, but toddlers prefer them peeled. Arrange them on a pretty plate. Scoop out a little well and put 1 knob of butter on each potato. Let the butter melt so that it looks succulent. Season with a little nutmeg and salt—try to get the new salt that comes from the Himalayas, which is pink and crunchy to eat; it's delicious. But top-quality sea salt is also good. Serve immediately. It's hot, smooth and creamy. Hey presto!

NB: everything goes well with potato. Try melting some Boursin or Chavroux cheese into it. Sprinkle a few cubes of York ham, and add some organic sesame, garlic oil, or tapenade (a rich olive paste popular in the Mediterranean) to the puree. Add a little foie gras for mom... or even better, a piece of goat's cheese. It's not so upmarket, but it's to die for!

Potato pancakes

Of Swiss or Alsatian origin, these country-style pancakes are made in a flash. You use a large frying pan and cook it in a single portion, which gives you the traditional "rösti." Children can make them themselves. You can add a handful of grated Swiss cheese, which is also delicious. These pancakes go very well with a small salad and a few cumin seeds on the edge of the plate (so that nobody feels forced to eat them). Once you've tried cumin, you'll acquire a taste for it. It's said that cumin gives breastmilk a lovely flavor…

· 2 lb (1 kg) potatoes
· 3 eggs
· 1 onion
· 3 tbsp chopped parsley (optional)
· Ground salt and pepper
· Nutmeg
· Sunflower oil

Grate the raw potatoes with a cheese grater. Dry them with a cloth or paper towel, and then put them in a bowl. Add the beaten eggs, the chopped onion, and a little parsley, salt, pepper, and nutmeg. Blend well. Heat the oil in a frying pan, and put 1 tablespoon of the mixture into it, spreading it with the back of a spoon to create the small pancakes. Turn the pancakes over so that they brown on both sides.

Another option: to make an au gratin version of it, you just need to grill the pancake for 2 minutes, with some Swiss cheese. Or you can get the real mountain atmosphere without that ingredient! Just take some country ham, three gherkins, and presto! It's ready!

Our potato gratin

Gratin—here we have a "mom's trick." Didn't your mom make any? This one is as soft as a teddy bear, and much lighter than a traditional gratin Dauphinois, because it has no cream or cheese. In our view, it's the genuine article, the only gratin. But, to be honest, it'll surprise you a little, owing to the subtle blend of flavors.

- 2 lb (1 kg) potatoes
- 4 cups milk
- 1 pinch ground cinnamon
- 1 pinch nutmeg
- Ground salt and pepper
- Butter

Preheat the oven to 400 °F (200 °F). Cut the potatoes into thin slices. Heat the milk with the cinnamon, nutmeg, salt, and pepper in a saucepan. When the mixture is hot, add the potatoes and cook for 15 minutes. Put the potatoes and milk into an oven dish. Add a few small knobs of butter. Put in a hot oven and bake for approximately 1 hour, until it melts. It's kid's stuff.

Double treat: wholewheat spaghetti and vegetable spaghettis

"My mom is the best cook in the world, because she knows how to make small macaroni with butter." Pasta and starch—of course, that's all they like! Once again you need the Japanese mandolin for this simple, tasty recipe. What's important is the mixture of textures. Wholewheat pasta tastes good when it's very soft. Vegetables have to be "al dente." If they're quickly and properly done, vegetables cook by themselves. There's no need to use two saucepans. By the time you've finished washing the children's hands, it's ready. Sprinkle with coarsely grated Parmesan—use it sparingly—and serve. And then, you can also impress your friends with this recipe when you invite them for supper. Try it!

- 9 oz (250 g) wholewheat spaghetti
- Salt
- 1 carrot
- 2 small zucchini
- 1 parsnip
- Olive oil
- Parmesan (optional)

Boil some water in a saucepan and throw in the spaghetti. Add a little salt. While it's cooking, use the mandolin to grate the vegetables lengthwise, to obtain long, even "spaghettis." Drain the pasta and put it back in the saucepan with a little oil. Add the raw vegetable spaghettis to the steaming pasta. Blend. Cover with a plate, so that they're completely airtight. Wait 5 minutes. Serve, and sprinkle with Parmesan, according to taste.

NB: this recipe is also very good with butter instead of cheese. Sometimes, children prefer its mellow flavor.

Spätzles

Related to noodles, spätzles are a delicious specialty from Alsace in France consisting of small, twisted pasta shapes that go well with butter. There's nothing more authentic than this! All you have to do is mention their name, and there's already a smile on your kids' lips. Some kids look at the shape of clouds in the sky and see animal forms, while others throw spoonfuls of what looks like melted lead into cold water to create funny droplets... Our preference is to throw spätzles into salted water and see them quiver, float, and swell. What will yours look like? Pebbles? Snakes? Moons? Small sausage shapes?

· 2 cups all-purpose flour
· 2 eggs + 1 yolk
· Salt
· 1/2 stick butter

Pour the all-purpose flour into a large bowl. Add the eggs, the yolk, some salt, and just enough water to obtain a smooth, thick consistency, mixing with a spoon. Work the mixture with your hands until it comes away from the sides of the bowl. Boil a saucepan of salted water. Spread out the mixture and cut out small sausage shapes. Throw them into the boiling water. As soon as the spätzles rise to the surface, remove them and rinse under the cold tap. Heat the butter in a frying pan and brown the spätzles gently. "What do we say to mom? I haven't heard the magic word..."

Risotto with lemon and Gorgonzola

Yes, risotto—it's very trendy, but what matters to us is that it will be a good dish to eat. This recipe is soft and creamy like rice pudding. It's so good that you can give it to babies—if anything, you'd add a vanilla pod and a very small amount of salt. Make a large amount of the risotto and finish the dish yourself. Don't have any qualms about the strong flavor of Gorgonzola; this is the ingredient that gives the recipe its character. It melts smoothly, it's sublime. The apparent pale color of this risotto reveals true character... *Molto buono.*

- 1 clove garlic
- 1 onion
- 1/2 stick butter
- 1 lemon
- 1 1/3 cups round rice (if possible special risotto rice, from Italian grocery stores)
- Vegetable bouillon (made from 1 cube)
- 1/2 cup crumbled Gorgonzola with Mascarpone

Chop the garlic and onion very finely, and then brown gently in butter in a saucepan. Remove the peel from the lemon and squeeze out the juice. Pour all these into the saucepan, together with the rice. Blend well over gentle heat until the grain is translucent. Cover with water and add the bouillon (made from a cube). Cook on low heat for 20 minutes, adding 2 cups water or more as you go, until the rice absorbs it all. Three minutes before the end of cooking, add the Gorgonzola and Mascarpone. Stir well, and serve when the cheeses have melted.

NB: if the result is too thick, adjust the texture by adding some more lemon juice.

Quick French fries

We had vowed: (1) that they wouldn't be hooked on French fries, (2) that deep-frozen French fries would never enter our house, (3) that we would not have a French fryer of the kind given on Mother's Day. Well? Let's not be prudish: we adore French fries too. If we continue to be perfectionists, it remains to be seen what we can give them to eat. Quite simply, these fries are cooked in the oven, and are served with tender friend chicken (1 between 2 children); they're well roasted with olive oil and a pinch of paprika.

• 2 lb (1 kg) potatoes with firm skins
• Olive oil
• Ground salt and pepper

Cut the potatoes into four or eight pieces into the shape of fries or, if you prefer, wedges. Wash and dry the potato pieces thoroughly with a clean cloth or paper towel. Preheat the oven to 425 °F (220 °C). Oil a baking sheet and arrange the fries over it. Baste them with oil, sprinkle with salt and a little pepper. Using your hands, you can gently "massage" the fries, so that they're thoroughly coated with oil. Bake in the oven for 20–25 minutes, turning them from time to time with a spatula.

International trends: the British eat French fries with vinegar, the Germans with mayonnaise, the Americans with ketchup, the Swedes with mustard. And how about you? Do you eat them on their own or dipped in something?

Meat
and small complete dishes

Moms' words :
Random thoughts and maxims

The quasi-controlled order in my house with its pastel colors has given way to the disturbing chaos of a cupboard that is collapsing under odd socks. Before I would go and see exhibitions at the drop of a hat... Or even Finnish films. I had the choice.
A mom who would almost feel remorse.

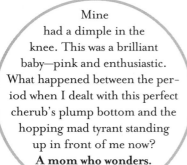

Mine had a dimple in the knee. This was a brilliant baby—pink and enthusiastic. What happened between the period when I dealt with this perfect cherub's plump bottom and the hopping mad tyrant standing up in front of me now?
A mom who wonders.

One evening, I sent my 4-year-old son to bed without supper. Was he going to one of hunger's Worst Circles from Hell? As a matter of fact, he slept very well. And the next day, everything was OK.
A mom who indulges in guilt.

Sometimes,
grown tired of their
capacity for resistance, I let
them invent their own dishes and
their combinations of flavors. But
on one condition: whoever made it,
eats it! The recipes are surreal, but it
works.

**A mom who has a flair for
being true to her word.**

There
was a day when I was at
the end of my tether after a
memorable succession of refusals
to eat and I ended up improvising a
supper for mermaids in the bath. I saw
my daughters, smiling, finish their plates
in the bubble bath. I wondered if I had
become incredibly inventive or had
quite simply gone crazy.

**A mom who tries to find
herself**

Shepherd's pie with vegetables

Shepherd's pies are the "in" thing, in restaurants everywhere... Without knowing it, would children find themselves in the midst of the latest trend? This coffeeshop food classic is extremely simple and gives you scope to be very creative. The concept of two layers snugly superimposed gives a feeling of cocooning. Serve it in small dishes, so that it doesn't look like school meals.

· 4 potatoes
· I carrot
· I tomato
· I parsnip (optional)
· I salad heart
· 4 slices of lamb
· I onion
· I clove garlic
· I tbsp olive oil
· Salt
· Salted butter (optional)
· A little grated cheese

Preheat the oven to 350 °F (180 °C). Peel and cut the vegetables into pieces. Steam them for 20 minutes. Cut the meat, the onion, and garlic into small pieces, and brown this mixture gently in oil. Add a little salt and cook gently for approximately 10 minutes, while stirring thoroughly. When the vegetables are cooked, pour a little of the cooking water into a bowl, drain the vegetables, and blend into a puree. You can add I knob of salted butter, if liked. Put one layer of meat and then the vegetables into each small ramekin. Add I tablespoon of the vegetable water and sprinkle with grated cheese. Bake in the oven for 10 minutes.

Baked ramekins

Our darlings. There's a false air of an educational school trip to the country-side: a woven basket, a carton of cream cheese, a dozen eggs from the hen house... It's pure and simple. A quick, unique concept that gives free rein to the imagination. You can devise your own combination or gain your ideas by memorizing everything in this list: "In my ramekins, I put..."

For Céleste (who doesn't like anything): egg, butter, salt.
For Hugo: egg, cream cheese, Swiss cheese, curry.
For Antoine: egg, cream cheese, Swiss cheese, ham.
For Basile: egg, cream cheese, Swiss cheese, tomato.
For Edgar (who eats anything and is always hungry): egg, cream cheese, Swiss cheese, potato, broccoli, peas...

Serves 1

• 1 egg
• 1 good tbsp cream cheese mixed with a little lemon juice
• 1 small tbsp of something else, according to taste
• Salt

Preheat the oven to 425 °F (220 °C). Put the ingredients in ramekins, layering them on top of each other, starting with a small spoonful of the cream cheese mixture. Bake in the oven for 6–7 minutes.

NB: we serve these with fingers of buttered bread or breadsticks dunked in warm, steaming egg yolk. No child can resist them!

Slice of bread topped with egg

This classic 1970s recipe has never disappointed us. It blows away children just as it impressed us in its time. Be simple and inventive in the evening when there's practically nothing left to eat in the refrigerator. With quails' eggs, you can create two eyes… and make a little face with ketchup. That's talent!

- Sandwich loaf (bread without crusts is firmer)
- Butter
- 1 small hen's egg or 2 quail's eggs, per person
- Salt
- Allspice
- Anything you have to hand for decoration purposes: cheese, cucumber, ketchup, ham, cherry tomatoes…

Preheat the oven to 425 °F (220 °C). Butter a firm slice from a sandwich loaf. Make a hole in the middle with the aid of a small glass, or with the top of a mineral water bottle if you're using quail's eggs. Remove the circle from the sandwich loaf. Put the bread on a nonstick plate or a baking sheet, and break the egg or eggs into the hole made in the slice of bread. Add a pinch of salt and a hint of allspice. Bake in the oven for 5–6 minutes. Decorate with ketchup and some vegetables— you could serve with raw vegetables and a sprinkling of salt, for example.

Browned breaded escalopes

There was a time when we considered escalopes something stodgy and outmoded. Perhaps they were a hazy childhood memory… We worked on our classics and changed our minds. Served with a good salad, they are a delicious meal for dads, too. Whether you make chicken or fish morsels, success is guaranteed: the crispy texture is a hit with our kids! Try different escalopes, from various kinds of melba toast (muesli, fiber, cereals, brioche), with spices, parmesan… Let your children go on a voyage of discovery. Their taste buds are more alert than you think! You won't be able to resist it either. Here's one idea: always leave half a lemon on the table—it can be used to season everything, the children will acquire a taste for it, and, without making a big deal about it, it contains Vitamin C.

Mild chicken curry

- Beaten egg
- Fine homemade breadcrumbs, made from melba toast
- Chicken breast
- Mixture of spices milder than curry, suitable for children
- Oil

Crispy chicken with tomato

- Beaten egg
- Breadcrumbs
- Diced fillet of fish
- Tomato pulp mixed without juice
- Parmesan
- Oil

Red beef meatballs

- Beaten egg
- Breadcrumbs
- Ground beef
- Thinly sliced red onion
- Paprika
- Oil

The basic recipe is the same for all three variations: prepare a small bowl of beaten egg and a small bowl of breadcrumbs; mix the basic ingredients, make some croquettes, dip them in the egg, roll them in the breadcrumbs, then fry in a little oil.

Mini cordon-bleu parcels

All the effort goes into making the meat parcels! Yes, it's true that the anti-meat brigade exists and that vegetarian children puff out their cheeks, which are as pink as the next kid's. Having said that, without overindulging in meat, it remains one of the pleasures of the table. Our children ask for more. They're all carnivores, we know! What's important is the quality and the proportions. This recipe remains faithful to the cordon-bleu principle, but has an Italian Saltimbocca twist. Take a wooden meat tenderizer, and away you go! Mom bashes a small escalope like a crazy woman! It helps her relax, so that's fantastic! After the age of 5, they can try it (before, you reckon?). The aim is to obtain a piece of meat which is as thin as paper, or nearly.

- 4 escalopes of very thin veal
- 4 slices of soft cheese (Leerdammer, Gouda, or another Swiss cheese...)
- Cherry tomatoes
- Gherkins (optional)
- Olive oil
- Salt
- Sauce (optional)
- String, and scissors with rounded points

Cut each escalope into four, and then roll up the portions with 1 slice of cheese. Don't forget to include a "surprise" in the center: a cherry tomato, a gherkin, a bit of cheese. Roll, tie up, and discuss sailors' knots. Add salt, and fry with a trickle of oil for 10 minutes. Serve plain or with a mild mustard, ketchup, and/or 1 trickle of lemon juice.

NB: what are the pros and cons of ketchup? They adore it, but don't make a habit of it. A good fresh tomato sauce with 1 lump of brown sugar is nice, too.

Sticky chicken

This is a wonderful combination of sweet and savory, which is really simple and sensational. You have to eat it with your fingers, of course! It's rewarding for mom, because the dish is always empty in less than two minutes. Feel free to add some marinade to the cooking: it'll evaporate but will give even more of a smooth and "sticky" texture. Fantastic!

· 6 chicken breasts
· 3 tbsp liquid honey
· 2 tbsp soy sauce
· I tbsp mild mustard
· 3 tbsp sunflower oil
· I pinch of mild pepper (optional)
· I pinch of light brown granulated sugar + extra for caramelizing (optional)

Cut the chicken breasts into thin strips. Mix all the other ingredients in a bowl, until you have a marinade. Put the chicken into the marinade and place in the refrigerator for at least I hour. Preheat the oven to 425 °F (220 °C). Put the chicken breasts on a baking sheet and bake them for 10 minutes. Take the dish out of the oven and turn over the strips. Add the rest of the marinade, sprinkle with a little pepper and sugar, according to taste, and cook for a further 10 minutes, until the chicken has thoroughly caramelized.

Children's sushis

Did you know that the art of sushi requires several years' apprenticeship? At least, for real Japanese chefs it does. But that doesn't prevent you from trying it at home, and inviting your children to take part in this hands on cooking class. The term "sushi" means a rice-based snack, with fish and vegetables added. In this recipe, we're suggesting a different variation of "maki sushi"—you can use spinach leaves, which are easier to find, as an alternative to the usual seaweed. However, our advice is to take the kids to a Japanese restaurant with an open kitchen— but only from the age of 4 upward—so that they can watch the chefs working at high speed. It would be even better if you have the opportunity to take them along to a self-service Japanese restaurant!

- 1/2 cup round rice
- 2 slices ultra-fine Serrano or Parma ham
- 1/2 cucumber
- 1 avocado
- Lemon juice
- Fresh spinach leaves or a roll of Japanese seaweed
- 1 carrot
- Soy sauce
- 1 pinch light brown sugar
- Horseradish sauce (optional)

Cook the rice as usual. Mold part of it into small sausage shapes (you can get the children to help). Using scissors, cut up the ham into even rectangles. Place these rectangles on top of the small rice sausage shapes. Cut the half cucumber and avocado into sticks, and sprinkle lemon juice over them. Make some more small rice sausage shapes, and push these sticks into them. If you use spinach leaves, rinse them in warm water to soften them. Wrap the spinach leaves or seaweed round the rice and arrange them on a plate, with the finely grated carrot. Dip these "maki sushis" in lightly sweetened soy sauce. Those of you who are brave enough can try these with horseradish sauce instead.

Tiny stew

This is adult fare for children—you'll witness their first protests at the sight of food served in sauce. Armed with a slate, and a blue apron, mom announces the inspiration: the dish of the day, the only dish on offer this evening, is inspired by Morocco! This stew is very mild and very fragrant. Its perfume wafting through the house will be the signal that it's time to sit down at table. While it's simmering, you'll have the time to do many other things with the children. Even so, make sure you notice the smell of burning when you're watching their favorite program with them just before supper...

· 1 cup dried apricots
· Olive oil
· 2 chopped onions
· 2 or 3 cloves chopped garlic
· 1 tsp ginger (optional)
· 1 tsp ground cinnamon
· 1_ lb (600 g) diced lamb or chicken
· 2 potatoes
· Ground salt and pepper
· Almonds, pistachios, coriander, pine nuts (optional)

Half an hour before starting this dish, put the dried apricots in a bowl and cover them with boiling water. Fry gently the onions, the garlic, and the spices in oil, and then fry the meat in a casserole dish. Peel the potatoes and cut them in two. Add the apricots, with their water, and the halved potatoes to the casserole; season with salt and pepper, and cook over moderate heat for 2–3 hours. Keep a watchful eye on this and add water if necessary. If you wish, you can add a few grilled almonds and chopped pistachios, coriander, or pine nuts at the end of cooking.

NB: our children have been raised with spices and garlic—if I may say that. I think you'll agree that it did them good. It's a question of habit, like olive oil, Gorgonzola, or cranberry juice. Sweet food is not the only pleasurable thing in life. Have faith in them, and introduce new foods gradually.

Pitta pizza

When Stephanie was pregnant with the twins, she had a craving for pizzas—at least three or four a day. She tried them all and was on familiar terms with at least four delivery people in her area. But in the end, this is the recipe that won her vote: a recipe she tried as she came across a somewhat empty refrigerator at 3a.m. The base is thin and crispy, as it is in Italy. And there's nothing more simple to make. The twins were born, and Stephanie is still making these pizzas, which is not always the case with things we adored when we were pregnant! The children can become little pizza makers and put anything they like on their pizza (ham, mozzarella, mushrooms, bacon cubes, egg, capers…). The bigger they get, the more they like unusual toppings. It seems that when they get to around 16–17 years of age, it's sheer madness! Our pizzas look pretty on the page, don't they?

· 2 pitta breads
· Tomato puree
· 4 fresh tomatoes
· 2 fresh mozzarellas
· Olive oil
· Oregano

First tip: put the pitta breads in the toaster, so that they swell a little, which makes them easy to cut in two across their width. Spread tomato puree over each half of bread. Slice the tomatoes and mozzarellas, and arrange them on the bread. Sprinkle with oil and oregano. Preheat the oven to 425 °F (220 °C). Second tip: bake in a hot oven for 20 minutes, and the ultra thin dough suddenly becomes very crispy. Serve immediately.

Island fisherman casserole

Here's an original recipe that is as easy as pie. It's a divine combination of tastes and flavors: exquisite fish, which is neither too sweet nor too salty, a journey of color with turmeric, the fragrance of basmati, and the freshness of mango. The game involves finding the name of the island fisherman and inventing a story about him: perhaps a fiancee, singing his song... It's crazy what a mom can do with a recipe! Children really like this casserole and a variation on the theme is fish with breadcrumbs or cooked in a court bouillon. Serve it in small individual bowls, which makes it look prettier.

- 1 cup coconut milk (1 standard tin)
- Juice and a little rind from 2 limes
- 1 tsp ground ginger
- 2 tsp turmeric
- Ground salt and pepper
- 1 1/2 lb (600 g) frozen, diced, fileted fish, or fresh filets
- 1 mango
- Basmati rice

Put the coconut milk with the lime rind and juice into a casserole dish or a stew-pan. Heat the dish, and then add the ginger and turmeric. Add a little salt and pepper. Check the seasoning and add spices, according to your taste and your children's. Poach the fish in this mixture for approximately 10 minutes, until it's cooked. Meanwhile, finely dice the uncooked mango, which you can either arrange raw on a warm dish, or make into mini-kebabs presented on toothpicks. Serve with basmati rice.

Desserts

Moms' words
Did I really say that?
Well, yes, actually…

Don't stuff your-self with bread!

Fish
is good
for your
memory.

Be
off with
you!

Carrots
add pretty
color to the
dish.

Don't
kick under
the table!

Did
you ask to
leave the
table?

It's good
because mom
made it!

Because
that's how
it is!

Sit
up straight.
The cat in front,
the mice behind.

You
have to eat
a little bit of
everything

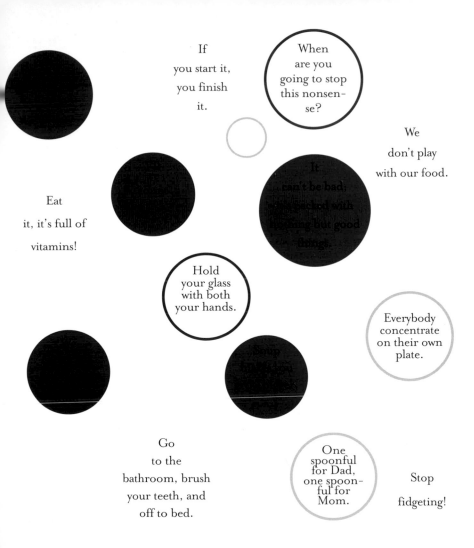

If
you start it,
you finish
it.

When
are you
going to stop
this nonsen-
se?

We
don't play
with our food.

Eat
it, it's full of
vitamins!

It
can't be bad,
it's packed with
nothing but good
things.

Hold
your glass
with both
your hands.

Everybody
concentrate
on their own
plate.

Soup
is what you
need.

Go
to the
bathroom, brush
your teeth, and
off to bed.

One
spoonful
for Dad,
one spoon-
ful for
Mom.

Stop
fidgeting!

Alsace apple tart

Ah! Desserts… They're not an end in themselves, but they're still the little extra that makes life more pleasant. Pastry making is chemistry, it's mathematics. Follow these recipes—they've been tried and tested for their effectiveness. Later, when you get into your stride, you'll find your own way to improvise. There's nothing easier than giving pleasure to people. These recipes smell good, they're comical, and they'll earn you the admiration of everyone. This particular tart melts in the mouth.

- 1 1/3 cup all-purpose flour with a raising agent (or all-purpose flour + 1/2 envelope baking powder)
- 1/3 cup superfine sugar
- 5 egg yolks
- 1 tbsp milk
- 1/2 stick butter, softened
- 5–6 fine apples using the pippin variety
- 1/2 cup vanilla sugar
- 1/2 cup cream cheese
- A little lemon juice
- 7 tsp ground almonds

Put 7/8 cup all-purpose flour, the baking powder if used, the superfine sugar, 2 egg yolks and the milk in a bowl. Blend with your fingers, until you obtain a thick mixture. Add the butter and the rest of the all-purpose flour. The mixture should be both smooth and light. Using your hands, spread out the mixture in the mold, while shaping the edge. Pierce it with a fork, so that it doesn't swell. Preheat the oven to 400 °F (200 °C). Peel the apples, cut them into quarters, and then arrange them over the mixture. Lightly split them lengthwise, so that they cook better. Bake in the oven for 25 minutes. Meanwhile, beat the remaining egg yolks, vanilla sugar, cream cheese, lemon juice, and ground almonds with a fork. Pour this mixture over the tart and bake for a further 10 minutes. Serve warm.

Smooth chocolate dessert

This is kind of an inspired quintessence of chocolate cake. It's perfect, and children like its strong chocolate taste, which isn't always the case… We've put it in the "ordinary" desserts section, but it also makes an excellent birthday cake: you just need to add a little decoration. Every time you make it there'll be someone who'll ask you for the recipe—guaranteed. You can make this masterpiece in a quarter of an hour (there aren't any stiffly beaten egg whites). The outside should be crunchy and the inside very smooth and creamy. It's important to keep a close eye on the cooking and to "under-cook" it slightly to obtain the melting texture, bordering on runny. Finally, a bit of advice about pastry making in general: if possible, make sure that the ingredients are at room temperature, by preparing them a little in advance.

· 7 oz (200 g) dark chocolate
· 1/2 stick butter (you can increase the quantity, it's always good…)
· 2/3 cup superfine sugar
· 3 eggs
· 5/8 all-purpose flour

Preheat the oven to 425 °F (220 °C). Melt the chocolate and the butter over low heat. Add the superfine sugar, allow it to cool a little, and then add the eggs and the all-purpose flour. Bake in the oven for 15–20 minutes. And hey presto!

Succulent layers

The trick here is to fill pretty glasses with layers of different mixtures, in order to arouse your children's curiosity and taste buds. It looks beautiful, it's very simple to make, and it's the in thing! Serve thoroughly chilled. Here are a few ideas that have already been tried and tested.

· Broken meringues
· Vanilla chestnut cream
· Cream cheese with a dash of lemon juice
· Milk chocolate shavings for decoration

· Crispy breakfast cereals
· Soft white cheese
· Apple or pear compote
· Small slices of apple for decoration

· Small broken cookies
· Vanilla cream
· Red fruits
· Fresh raspberries for decoration

· Beaten petits suisses or other low fat soft cheese
· Mashed banana
· Quince jello
· Caramelized rice souffle
· 1 slice of banana for decoration.

This isn't really a recipe — you just need to layer the ingredients. All the same—one word about the "banana quince" mix: it was invented one "bad tummy" evening to make little tummies better. This ultra simple dessert has become a classic at our home. You should use good jello (with a lot of pectin… or use apple, which is also good) and the result will be perfect. Moreover, we moms always finish any that are left over. This is fantastic in the evening, in bed with a good thriller. The ideal proportions are 1 banana to 3 tablespoons of quince jello, blended in the juicer.

Mini-pancakes with cream cheese, vanilla sugar, and stewed fruits

These irreplaceable pancakes are mouthwatering, golden brown, and light. The more you make them, the more you like them. You'll quickly get the hang of preparing them. It's easier if you have a frying pan suitable for small, thick pancakes. When we're making them, we devour them as we go along on the quiet, before sitting down at table. (This really isn't polite, but that's too bad— they simply taste too good!) They come under the heading of desserts, but you can serve them on Sunday evening during a "chill out" type of weekend, when you don't want to make life difficult for yourself. They're very soft with compotes. Maple syrup suits this recipe to perfection. Children adore the simplicity of these pancakes. We like their lightness— they don't have too much flour in them.

- Generous 1 cup thick soft white cheese (the curd variety: very well strained)
- 4 tbsp all-purpose flour
- 1 egg + 1 yolk
- 2 envelopes vanilla sugar
- 1 pinch salt
- Oil

Mix the soft white cheese, the all-purpose flour, the whole egg, and the yolk, 1 envelope vanilla sugar, and the salt in a bowl. Heat a little oil in a large frying pan, and pour in tablespoonfuls of this mixture, spacing them out well. As soon as the pancakes are lightly browned (this happens very quickly), turn them over. Sprinkle them with the rest of the vanilla sugar and keep them warm. Serve them with apple compote.

Here are a few examples of compotes: dried fruits (apricots, figs, prunes) in winter; apricot and vanilla, and of course apples and pears. Don't cook the fresh fruits for very long, and drain them through a conical strainer.

Au pair's cream cheese tart

This cousin of the cheesecake is light, sweet, and rather sharp at the same time. A young au pair from east of the Rhine gave me the recipe; her homesickness made her grouchy. I've never found this anywhere else (the recipe, not the grouchiness). I make it just to please her, and I forgive you, Fräulein. There's a knack to this: you need to be handy with the whisk, to remove the mixture from the heat, and then beat it again. It is really child's play, and to be quite honest, this tart is really extraordinary!

- 7 oz (200 g) cookies of the digestive variety (graham crackers)
- 5/8 stick butter
- 2 envelopes vanilla dessert (about 3 oz / 80 g in all (to be found in the pastry section, with the tart bases)
- 7/8 cup superfine sugar
- 2 cups cold milk
- 1 lb 10 oz (750 g) smooth soft white cheese, 40% fat
- 3 eggs

Mix the broken cookies and the butter, and press this mixture into a mold with a removable base. Mix the vanilla dessert with half of the sugar and half of the milk. Place to one side. Bring the rest of the milk to the boil, reserving 1 tsp of it. Remove from the heat, and add the mixture to the dessert. Beat well and return it to the heat while stirring it until it boils. Remove from the heat and blend the mixture with the soft white cheese. Return it to the heat, stirring constantly until it boils, and then remove from the heat. Separate the egg whites from the yolks. Stiffly beat the whites and add them to this mixture, with the rest of the superfine sugar. After you've obtained a smooth cream, pour it into the mold, over the mixture. Preheat the oven to 375 °F (190 °C). Using a brush, spread a little yolk mixed with the reserved milk over the cake. Bake in the oven for 1 hour. When you take it out of the oven, loosen the mixture from the side of the mold. Let it cool and put it in the refrigerator. Serve thoroughly chilled.

Tartlets and tarts

Tart pastry often poses quite a tiresome technical problem. It's either soft, moist, and impossible to cut into attractive portions, or it's so powdery that it crumbles before it goes anywhere near the mold... It's a real pain. What if there were only one pastry recipe that is crunchy, firm, sweet, and goes well with everything? Well, here it is. Rest assured, it's easy to make. It's incomparable with raw fruits in spring: strawberries, red currants... We adore it served in tartlets, garnished with chestnut cream, with lemon curd. As far as its performance as a classic fruit tart is concerned, it's the ultimate.

- 1 1/8 sticks butter
- 5 tbsp superfine sugar
- 2 1/2 cups all-purpose flour
- 1 egg
- 1 pinch salt
- Decoration of your choice
- Cream (optional)
- Lemon juice (optional)

Blend the butter and superfine sugar to obtain a frothy mixture. Add the all-purpose flour, the egg, and the salt. Mix well. Preheat the oven to 400 °F (200 °C). Roll out the dough with a floured rolling pin, cut out small circles with a glass or a pastry cutter, and put the dough into small nonstick molds. Bake in the oven for 8–10 minutes, making sure that they don't brown too much. Decorate with the fruits of your choice, accompanied by cream according to taste, to obtain the "petit-four" effect. To make a large, classic fruit tart (apples, pears, plums...), bake the tart base for 10 minutes, and then add the diced fruit. Sprinkle with lemon juice and superfine sugar, and then bake in the oven for a further 20 minutes.

Gateau moistened with fruits

Ready in a flash, this is the fruit dessert par excellence. It's as familiar as an old family friend, tender, reassuring, and tasty. It should be served with a spoon. It varies every time you make it, and it's good every time. Dark red plums full of juice, cherries, pears, or apples—anything goes. When it's ready, it's devoured in less than two minutes… An indispensable gateau for any perfect mom.

- 2 lb (1 kg) fruits, of your choice
- 4 tbsp all-purpose flour
- 1 tsp yeast
- 4 tbsp milk
- 7 tbsp superfine sugar
- 2 tbsp oil
- 2 eggs
- 1 pinch salt

Preheat the oven to 425 °F (220 °C). Peel the fruits, cut them up if they're big, and put them on a baking sheet, approximately 7 inches (18 cm) in diameter. Mix the other ingredients in a bowl until you obtain a smooth mixture. If using active dry yeast, follow the maker's instructions. Pour this mixture over the fruits and blend a little. Bake in the oven for 35–40 minutes.

Banoffee pie

"Ban" for banana, "offee" for toffee: this is a wacky delight that was introduced by a British babysitter, who's as thin as a rake despite the 2,500 calories in each portion. This dish is a food lover's paradise which should be savored at least once in a lifetime. Our little darlings like it unconditionally. We like it too, it has to be said. And then, as our babysitter would say so prettily: "Life is too short to be thin, darling." The incomparable taste of the gently cooked condensed milk, the softness of the banana and the appearance of the cream… To die for.

· 2 cans sweetened condensed milk (about 27 fl oz in all)
· 9 oz (250 g) chocolate cookies, of the digestive or Granola variety
· 7/8 stick butter, softened
· 3 bananas
· 8 oz (250 g) whipping cream
· Chocolate powder for the decoration

Cook the sweetened condensed milk by placing the two cans in a large saucepan of water without opening them and boiling for 1 hour. Be sure to keep an eye on the water level – if the can gets too much direct heat, the can could explode. Mix the cookies and blend them with the butter. Spread this mixture into a round mold approximately 7 inches (18 cm) in diameter, and pour the cooked condensed milk over it. When this mixture has thoroughly cooled, arrange the sliced bananas over the milk, cover with the whipped cream and sprinkle with chocolate powder. Put in the refrigerator. Serve thoroughly chilled.

Grated apples with rosemary honey and orange

This very simple little dessert is an interpretation of the traditional oven-baked apple dish. We find it much more appetizing and it doesn't look so crinkly. The three minutes and twelve hundredths of a second you lose when you grate the apple is gained during the cooking, which is almost symbolic as it's so quick. Savor the green of the rosemary (the more foolhardy among you can eat the little branch when you take the dish out of the oven) and the taste of the honey—it's simple and they complement each other perfectly.

· 4 apples
· Butter for greasing dish
· 1 branch fresh rosemary
· 3 tbsp rosemary honey
· 2 tbsp orange blossom water
· Juice of 1 orange
· 1 handful flaked almonds

Preheat the oven to 425 °F (220 °C). Peel the apples and grate them, if possible with a Japanese mandolin (this will give you a more consistent result). Put the grated apple in a buttered, oval oven dish. Arrange the rosemary branch on top. Pour the honey, the orange blossom water, and the orange juice over it. Bake in the oven for 5–6 minutes. Decorate with the flaked almonds and serve hot.

N.B.: for the height of decadence—you can add a scoop of vanilla ice cream.

Grandma's crystallized apples and quick custard

To be honest, it's all in the title, and it's true to say that it doesn't look very appetizing! You've heard it all before—things like "aunt what's-her-name's favorite" and "grandma's method." But this recipe really was passed down to us by one of our grandmothers and it's absolutely fabulous. There's no reason to pussyfoot around. It's like a fruit pastry, only better. I love you, grandma…

For the crystallized apples

· 4 1/2 lb (2 kg) stewed apples (ideally, using mixed varieties)
· 2 tbsp water
· 2 vanilla pods
· 1 1/3 cups white sugar
· 1/2 stick butter

For the custard

· 2 cups cream cheese
· A little lemon juice
· 1 tbsp superfine sugar
· 3 egg yolks
· Pure vanilla powder (without additives or sugar), or 1 large vanilla pod

A day in advance, peel the apples and cut them into small strips. Put them in a saucepan or a dish with 2 tablespoons of water and the vanilla pods. Add the white sugar and blend. Cook over very low heat for approximately 4 hours. The apples should be transparent and crystallized. Add the butter.
Place in a mold

and put in the refrigerator. The next day, turn out of the mold and serve with a quick custard that our babies have adored since they cut their first tooth. To make the custard, heat the cream cheese, lemon juice, and superfine sugar gently in a saucepan. Add the yolks and the vanilla, and stir until the mixture thickens. Put it in the refrigerator and stir regularly.

Gateau supreme with coconut

Sweetened condensed milk is one of our favorite ingredients. We've probably been influenced by the little hard candies of our childhood, eaten at recess or during a skiing vacation. This incomparable taste comes in very handy in the kitchen. It gives real creaminess and a sense of elegance to anything it comes in contact with. Here's the proof.

- 1 cup grated coconut
- 1 2/3 cups sweetened condensed milk
- 2 1/2 cups fresh milk
- 3 eggs
- Liquid caramel, or 1/2 cup superfine sugar + 2/3 cup water

Preheat the oven to 400 °F (200 °C). Put the coconut, the sweetened condensed milk, the milk, and the eggs in a food processor and whizz for 5 minutes. Pour the mixture into a loaf tin, or a deep cake pan approximately 7 inches (18 cm) in diameter. Bake in the oven for 40 minutes. Wait until the gateau has cooled down before you turn it out of the mold. Put it in the refrigerator and serve it thoroughly chilled, first topping it with liquid caramel. Either buy the caramel from a store, or make it yourself by melting the superfine sugar in 2/3 cup water for 10 minutes.

Soft dessert with lemon

Lemon, like apples, is a durable source of inspiration for moms. We always have a lemon to hand and children like its sharpness and color. It's simple, it's pretty, and it's not expensive. What an abundance of qualities! And what about this recipe? It's partly warm mousse and partly gateau—almost a tart… it's a pudding anyway. Try to make it in an oval oven mold, as they did in the past. It's quick to make, mouthwatering, and not stodgy. It's a light, souffle type of dessert, which has to be eaten immediately.

- 2 lemons
- 3 eggs—whites separated from their yolks
- 1 cup superfine sugar
- 1/2 cup all-purpose flour
- 1/2 stick butter, softened
- generous 1 cup milk
- Confectioner's sugar for decoration

Remove the rind from the lemons and squeeze out the juice. Beat the yolks with half the superfine sugar in a food processor to obtain a thick white cream. Add the all-purpose flour, the butter, the rinds and lemon juice, and then the milk. Beat for a further 2 minutes, to obtain a consistent mixture. Beat the egg whites stiffly while incorporating the rest of the superfine sugar. Blend the two mixtures. Preheat the oven to 375 °F (190 °C). Put the mixture into a large, but not too high, oval mold. Bake in the oven for 25—30 minutes. Serve at room temperature, sprinkled with confectioner's sugar.

Mom's iced strawberry gateau

This is a simple, sophisticated recipe that is a hit with everybody at chic supper parties! It's a well-known fact that children love ice cream, but not everybody has an ice-cream maker. Sometimes, we're even downright anti gadgets as they clutter up our workspace. You may already have a juicer, a waffle iron, a sauceboat, and that's not all... It was love at first sight when we tasted the sharpness of this ice cream. Mom's strawberry gateau is the ideal marriage of the pure whiteness of the ice cream and the redness of the ripe strawberries, bursting with joy. You mix it all with small pieces of crunchy meringues. It's delicious.

· 12 petits-suisses or similar cream cheeses
· Juice of 1 lemon
· 4 tbsp superfine sugar
· 2 large meringues
· 2 lb (1 kg) strawberries

Mix the petits-suisses or other cream cheeses with the lemon juice and sugar. Break the meringues into pieces. Wash the strawberries, and set a few aside for the decoration, and also some meringue pieces. Cut the remaining strawberries into small pieces. Blend the mixture in a bowl and transfer to a round container and put in the freezer. Wait half a day, and then turn out of the mold and decorate. This dessert should be taken out shortly before it's served, so that it can be enjoyed very chilled, but soft.

Snacks, parties,
and breakfasts

A bit of advice between friends

Don't take on too much. You can so easily have a psychosomatic reaction! Your back's killing you; you have a lump in your throat, and mouth ulcers and red blotches on your skin... Your job as mom shouldn't completely transform you like this. Get worked up, then chill out. Join a kick boxing, all-in wrestling, or fencing course—or choose a Gregorian chant choir. What's important is to shrug off the mild irritations of the day... away from your children.

You're at the end of your patience? No more time left for yourself? No more time to laugh at a stupid film? In the evening, do you collapse in a heap to avoid blowing your top? Take heart, it's normal. You're just normal. normal.

Does
a very strong foster
mother instinct lie dormant in
you? Did you know that children
are not the ideal audience for your large
dish of chili con carne, your chestnut
gateau, and your sinful chocolate cakes.
Instead of children, have a male student
friend handy, aged 18–22 years, whom you
invite on a regular basis. His insatiable
appetite and his unconditional praise will
hearten you. He'll wolf everything
down with gusto and will be a
role model for your chil-
dren. Great!

My
little daughter some-
times asks me: "Say, mom, if
Cinderella hadn't helped in the kitchen, she would never have met Prince
Charming, would she? So what would she
have done then? Nothing?"
I'm a little afraid that if I tell her too many
fairy tales such as this one, I'll mess up
my little princess's love life…
Actually, I think I have to chill
out about that.

Light cake with banana and white icing

You can sometimes blame the banana for falling to pieces during cooking. It's a bit unfair. What can you say about bananas flambe, eh? And about this cake, then! It's stating the obvious to say that it's sufficient unto itself and keeps very well in a metal container. As for its special icing—its slightly acid sweet flavor is an inspiration and goes well with everything tasty: spices, carrot cake…

For the cake

- 3 bananas
- 4 tbsp water
- 7/8 stick butter, softened
- 1 cup superfine sugar
- 2 eggs
- 2 cups all-purpose flour with raising agent
- 1/2 tsp baking soda
- 1 pinch salt

For the icing

- 7 oz (190 g) cream cheese
- 1 1/3 cup confectioner's sugar
- 2 tsp lemon juice

Preheat the oven to 400 °F (200 °C). Crush the bananas in a bowl and add 4 tablespoons of water. In another bowl, mix the butter with the superfine sugar until you obtain a white cream. Add the beaten eggs, the bananas, the all-purpose flour, the raising agent, and the salt. Don't blend too much. Pour the mixture into a loaf tin and bake in the oven for 40 minutes. To make the icing, beat the cream cheese with an electric beater, and then add the confectioner's sugar and the lemon juice. Continue to beat until the mixture is smooth. Wait until the cake has thoroughly cooled before you ice it.

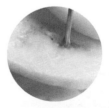

Welcome cake with orange blossom

Its old fashioned name is taken from a middle class cookbook that is a touch retro. It's a tea room classic for spruce ladies of the 1950s. We've adapted it a bit, after numerous attempts, and to be honest, we adore it. For all that, you're not obliged to get your hair curlers out! But it'll turn you into a charming mom… it's quick to make, and it's unpretentious. It's always smooth and creamy, and is like a security blanket. It has an air of false modesty. All our friends are already making it, without being obvious about it. It's an adorable recipe that every mom treasures in her secret diary.

- 6 eggs
- 1 1/3 cups superfine sugar
- 3 tbsp orange blossom water
- 1 1/3 cups all-purpose flour
- 1 1/3 cups cornstarch
- 1 1/2 sticks butter, softened

Preheat the oven to 375 °F (190 °C). Beat the whole eggs and the superfine sugar until you obtain a very frothy, pale yellow mixture. Add the orange blossom water, then the all-purpose flour, the cornstarch, and the butter. Blend well, pour into a mold, and bake in the oven for 20–30 minutes. It's delicious with custard or quite simply with whipped cream.

Chocolate cookies

Everybody likes cookies—these nice little treats you can take anywhere. It's worth making them yourself. Here are two different recipes—one is crunchy and the other one melts in the mouth. Cookies keep very well in a metal container.

Oat cookies and chocolate
- 1/2 stick butter
- Generous 1/2 cup white sugar or superfine brown sugar
- 1 beaten egg
- 1/2 cup all-purpose flour with raising agent (or all-purpose flour + 1 tsp baking powder)
- Generous 1 cup oatmeal
- 1 pinch salt
- cup milk chocolate chips or a 6 oz (170 g) bar of chocolate broken into pieces

Fantastic cookies with white chocolate
- 1 1/8 sticks butter
- 1/2 cup superfine white sugar
- 1 beaten egg
- 1 1/2 cups all-purpose flour
- 1/2 envelope baking powder
- 1 pinch salt
- 7 oz (200 g) white chocolate cut into small pieces

For both kinds, start by mixing the butter and the sugar until you have a pale cream. Add the other ingredients, leaving the chocolate chips or small pieces of chocolate to last. Preheat the oven to 400 °F (200 °C). Arrange small, well-spaced heaps on a buttered cookie sheet. Flatten them gently with the back of a spoon—don't overdo it. Bake in the oven for 8–10 minutes.

Quick flapjacks

British moms each have their own recipe. It's their secret... We adore this recipe, which was pinched from our friend Imogen, who makes them in a flash for her four sons when they come home from a cricket or football match in the rain. Generally, the flapjacks have all gone by the evening.

• 1 1/2 sticks butter or margarine
• 2/3 cups superfine brown sugar
• 1 tbsp British golden syrup (or dark or light molasses, or cane syrup, or corn syrup)
• 1 1/3 cups oatmeal
• 2/3 cup raisins (optional)

Preheat the oven to 375 °F (190 °C).. Mix the butter or margarine with the superfine brown sugar and the golden syrup (or molasses, or other syrup), and warm over low heat. Add the oatmeal and blend well. Pour the mixture onto a rectangular baking sheet and press down thoroughly. As a variation on the theme, you can add 2/3 cup raisins to the basic mixture. Bake in the oven for 20 minutes, until the mixture is thoroughly browned.

Be careful it doesn't overcook or you'll find that the flapjacks will be too hard. Leave to cool for a few minutes and cut it up into diamond shapes or triangles.

Mouthwatering crunchy crumble with cream

We've revisited this classic dish from Alsace in France and given it a creamy twist. This brioche consists of three superimposed mixtures, with different and complementary tastes and textures. But be careful! There's cinnamon, and there's cinnamon… Before buying it, smell it: it should be sweet and fruity. Ideally, prepare the raised pastry the day before, so that you can treat yourself to a sleep-in the next day—then all you'll have to do is put it in the oven. As far as I know, the sleep-in notion applies when you have children under 4 years old…

- 3 cups all-purpose flour
- 1/2 cup superfine sugar
- 1 pinch salt
- 3 tsp instant baker's yeast
- 1 cup milk
- 1 1/8 sticks butter, softened
- 2 eggs
- 3 tbsp liquid cream
- 1 envelope vanilla sugar
- 1 tsp ground cinnamon

Mix 2 cups of the all-purpose flour, 2 tbsp superfine sugar, the salt, and the baker's yeast in a large bowl. If using active dry yeast follow the maker's instructions. Warm the milk and add it to the mixture while kneading the dough. Add 1/2 stick butter and 1 beaten egg, and blend until you obtain a flexible mixture. Remove it from the bowl and knead on a board for approximately 10 minutes; it should be supple and consistent. If it's sticky, add a little more all-purpose flour. Mold it into a ball and cover it with a cloth. Leave it to raise for 1 hour, away from drafts and heat. Preheat the oven to 425 °F (220 °C). Line a round mold with the dough. Beat the remaining egg with the cream and the rest of the superfine sugar, and then spread this mixture over the raised pastry. Put the rest of the butter and the all-purpose flour, the vanilla sugar, and the cinnamon in a bowl. Blend with your fingertips until you obtain a crumble mixture, which you press down over the cream. Bake in the oven for 30 minutes. Serve warm or cold.

Fruited bread slices

In this recipe, everything is raw and fresh. Inspired by Budwig cream, advocated by Dr. Kousmine, who recommended cereals and raw foods, and a great classic of Swiss gastronomy—like muesli—this bread slice is a meal in itself. It's ideal after a long walk in the mountains! You'll think you're Heidi. Red cheeks and a bowl of oxygen... Thanks, mom! It's also great as a complete breakfast.

· 1 apple
· 1/2 cup filberts
· A few strawberries or white grapes
· Superfine brown sugar or liquid honey
· Ground cinnamon
· 3 tbsp smooth soft white cheese
· 1 trickle lemon juice
· 4 large slices of farmhouse bread
· 1 banana

After rubbing and cleaning the apple thoroughly, grate it with its skin on. Roughly chop the filberts—or use a small coffee mill to do the trick. Keep back a few fruits for decoration. In a bowl, mix the grated apple, the chopped filberts, and the rest of the strawberries or white grapes, in small pieces. Add superfine sugar or honey, and some cinnamon, according to taste. Lastly, add the soft white cheese. Stir gently, until you have a consistent mixture. Add the lemon juice. Spread this mixture over the slices of bread. Decorate with small slices of banana. Finally, decorate with the fruits you set aside.

Cooking workshop: "Christmas cookies"

At the age of 5, Mozart started composing. Before his fifth birthday, Louis XIV was crowned king and began his reign. At the age of 4, Freud was already advanced for his age. Yes… definitely. So, why not make your children into brilliant little pastry makers? They'll like making shapes with the pastry cutter, and arranging their treasures delicately in a container or hanging them on the Christmas tree. A cooking workshop will keep them busy. Great! They'll roll up their sleeves and knead with their hands, as in bygone days. Each country has its Christmas traditions. What's important is to establish a ritual, with very distinctive tastes and flavors. Try sticking cloves into oranges and putting them on a radiator. Hang pictures decorated by the children in the windows. Improvise…

Butterbredla butter cookies (it's another Alsatian dish)

- 2 1/2 sticks butter, softened
- Generous 1 cup superfine sugar
- Vanilla sugar
- 4 cups all-purpose flour
- 2 eggs + 1 yolk for glazing

Cinnamon cookies

- 2 1/2 sticks butter, softened
- Generous 1 cup superfine sugar
- 4 cups all-purpose flour
- 1 tbsp ground cinnamon
- Rinds of 1 lemon and 1 orange
- 3 eggs + 1 yolk for glazing purposes

The day before, mix all the ingredients with the exception of the yolk, and blend them thoroughly, until you obtain a flexible and consistent dough. Roll it into a ball and place in the refrigerator overnight. On the same day, roll out the dough thinly with a rolling pin, and cut out various shapes with a pastry cutter. Preheat the oven to 400 °F (200 °C). Using a brush, spread the egg yolk over the cookies to brown them. Bake in the oven for 10–15 minutes.

Cooking workshop: "coconut mice"

Here's another idea for a children's workshop. Honestly, they'll love those mice! They've been made over and over again—each time they invite their friends over, or to give a decorative touch to a gloomy afternoon. They never get bored. The more you make, the more inventive you'll become with the things you choose to decorate them. It's a real joy to see the different mouse personalities emerging... It works every time!

· 4 1/2 cups confectioner's sugar
· 2 1/3 cups sweetened condensed milk
· 2 1/2 cups grated coconut
· Green food coloring
· Licorice lengths for the tail
· Silver balls for the eyes
· Colored lozenges for the ears
· Anything you can think of for the decoration...

Mix the confectioner's sugar and the sweetened condensed milk in a large bowl. Add the coconut and blend well. Divide the mixture into 2 bowls. Put a few drops of green coloring into each, and add 3 more drops into one of these bowls, to obtain two shades of color. Put some teaspoons and coffee spoons in hot water, to avoid the mixture sticking, and then shape the mice with them. Invite the children to decorate their mice. Leave the mice to dry for 1 hour before eating them.

Tip: if you don't have any confectioner's sugar, it's useful to know that you can make it by passing some ordinary sugar through a blender.

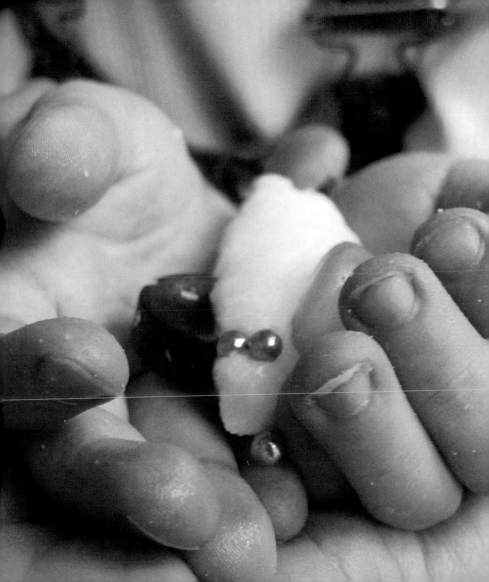

Small mouthfuls, balls, and croquettes

No, it's not the title of an animated cartoon. It's just an original way to become a confectioner, with simple little ideas to decorate a table and sweet things to snack on. And it's a good excuse for children to get their hands dirty. These are also ideal for adults when served with coffee. Everyone enjoys the comical variety of these sweet pearls.

Coconut croquettes

· I cup sweetened condensed milk
· I 1/2 cups grated coconut

Oriental carrot mouthfuls

· I lb (500 g) carrots
· I cup superfine sugar
· I cup water
· Juice of I lemon
· I pinch nutmeg
· I pinch ground cinnamon
· I pinch ground ginger
· 1/2 cup ground filberts

Chocolate balls with puffed rice

· 1/2 stick margarine
· 8 large marshmallows
· 2 oz (50 g) milk chocolate
· 2 envelopes vanilla sugar
· 3 oz (90 g) puffed rice (your choice of breakfast cereal)

Coconut croquettes: mix the sweetened condensed milk with the coconut (set some aside for the decoration). The mixture should be thick. Mold into croquettes and roll them in the rest of the coconut.

Oriental carrot mouthfuls: peel and grate the carrots. Make a syrup with the superfine sugar and water. Add the lemon juice and spices. Stir in the carrots and the ground filberts. Cook over low heat in a saucepan for 45 minutes. Leave to cool, and then mold into very firm balls.

Chocolate balls with puffed rice: melt the margarine and the marshmallows. Add the chocolate and the vanilla sugar. Stir. When you obtain a smooth consistency, add the puffed rice. Mold into balls and allow to cool.

Strawberry syrup Princess Gateau

Here's an aesthetic necessity: the few drops of red food coloring we indulge ourselves in. Purists will use beet juice. Whatever you use, this marble cake should be pink! Lose yourself in the kitsch taste of your little girls, with fluffy mules, mauve nail polish, and a handbag with sequins. It's over to you, my Celeste, forever.

- 1 1/2 cups butter, softened + extra for the mold
- 1 1/2 cups superfine sugar
- 3 eggs
- 1 1/3 cups all-purpose flour with raising agent (or ordinary flour + 2 tsp yeast)
- 2 tbsp strawberry syrup
- Red food coloring
- 1 envelope vanilla sugar

Blend the butter and the superfine sugar into a frothy mixture. Add the eggs. Gradually add the all-purpose flour, and the yeast if you wish, to the mixture while blending. If using active dry yeast follow the maker's instructions. Divide the mixture in two: put 1/3 of it into a small bowl, and the remaining 2/3 into a larger bowl. In the smaller bowl, add the strawberry syrup and a few drops of coloring to obtain the color you like (the gateau fades during cooking). Put the vanilla sugar in the other bowl. Preheat the oven to 400 °F (200 °C). Butter a loaf tin. Put some of the vanilla mixture into it, and then a little of the strawberry mixture. Alternate each mixture in this way, wherever your imagination takes you. Bake in the oven for 30–35 minutes, until the end of a knife inserted in the center of the gateau emerges dry. Turn it out of its mold and leave to cool on a grid. Serve with the maximum amount of decoration if it's for a party… It's perfect without decoration too.

Knights' gateau

After that pink, sheer delight, in our concern for symmetry we were tempted by a "boy's" cake. We've even imagined a gateau for a "little soldier with a military air." It was a muscular, drab olive color. Er… Who wants an drab olive gateau? It's too gimmicky. We decided against it. May all the little superheroes of the world forgive us, even if their propensity for fighting sometimes makes us smile. The little guys are invited to the knights' after-school snack (without their submachine guns). The great idea about this gateau is that quite simply you use brownie squares in the same way as building bricks. Our recipe based on this classic was given to us by a friend who's the mother of three children in New York. She's always in a hurry, always perfect, and disorganized at the same time. Just like the rest of us.

- 7 oz (200 g) dark chocolate
- 1 stick butter + extra for the mold
- 4 eggs
- 1 pinch salt
- 1 1/2 cups superfine sugar
- Liquid natural vanilla
- 7/8 cup all-purpose flour
- 2/3 cup walnuts, filberts, or almonds, shelled
- 1 slab chocolate for the doors, the windows, or the slits
- 4 chocolate cookies—use chocolate fingers for the drawbridge
- Birthday candles
- 1 toothpick to make the flag

Preheat the oven to 400 °F (200 °C). Melt the dark chocolate and the butter in a large saucepan. Remove from the heat. Add the eggs, one by one, and the salt. Blend well and add the superfine sugar. The mixture should turn creamy. Add a few drops of vanilla, the all-purpose flour, and the nuts. Put the mixture into a buttered square mold and bake in the oven for approximately 20 minutes. Turn out of the mold, leave to cool on a grid, and cut the gateau into cubes to build the castle. Add the decorations.

Magic cake

Mouthwatering cookies, a soft and light meringue—in some ways this gateau represents our mascot. It's pretty and it's a bluff. The children choose: a sugared almond fairy or a bellflower fairy... We like its sweet flavor, its naivete, its look of sheer indulgence: it's a genuine Sunday gateau to eat with our little fairies, together with a large bowl of strawberries. To die for! What shall we choose for the top? Sugar by way of a magical cure? A plastic black and white couple? A dog that shakes its head as they do when they're in the back of cars? A cuddly minibear toy? A bather closing his eyes? A photo of mom? (No, just kidding...).

For the pastry

· 1/2 cup superfine sugar
· 1 1/8 sticks butter
· 4 beaten yolks
· 4 tbsp milk
· 1/2 cup all-purpose flour with raising agent
  (or ordinary flour + 1 tsp baking powder)

Pour la garniture

· 4 egg whites
· 1 pinch salt
· Vanilla extract
· 1/2 cup superfine sugar
· Fairies, sugared almonds, flowers, petals,
  whipped cream and strawberries... for the
  decoration

Beat the superfine sugar and the butter together. Add the beaten yolks, milk, the all-purpose flour, and the baking powder if used. Blend well and pour this mixture into a round mold. Preheat the oven to 375 °F (190 °C). Make a meringue by beating the egg whites into a mousse. Add the salt, the vanilla extract, and the superfine sugar. Beat until the mousse is very shiny. Pour it onto the cake mixture and bake in the oven for 30 minutes. The meringue should be pale. Decorate, for example with whipped cream and strawberries, and serve warm.

Children's buffet

For a children's after-school treat, here's an attractive alternative to candies. Here are perfect raw vegetables too, for a summer meal that is fresh and convivial. Above all, you need to be continually inventive with your sauces, and to be clever with your choice of proteins: mini-sausages, rolled/crinkly ham, Gruyere cubes, hardboiled quails' eggs. For sweet food, you're spoiled for choice with these sugary recipes and croquettes... Consider buying some little bags for their friends to take away with them, containing stickers, very cheap toys, balloons, rapidly printed digital photos of the party... The other moms will be glad to see something other than candies!

Vegetables

· Carrots
· Artichokes
· Cucumber
· Horseradish
· Chicory

Sauces

· Thick soft white cheese
· Lemon
· Mustard seed
· Top quality salt

Prepare all the vegetables in very small portions, if possible by cutting them into sticks that are easy to handle, similar to fingers of bread that they can dunk in the sauces.

Variations on the sauce theme: Mediterranean: light mayonnaise with garlic. American: yogurt + ketchup. Oriental: sesame cream + blended avocado + lemon juice. British: yogurt + 1 envelope of dried onion soup. Fisherman: cream cheese made from ewes' milk + 3 tablespoons taramasalata. Squirrel: melted cheese of the "Laughing Cow" variety + cream cheese + lemon juice + ground filberts. Blue: beaten Roquefort cream + yogurt. Red: yogurt + 1 cooked red beet + mild mustard + sunflower oil.

Iced chocolate gateau balls

"Mom, the ice cream is too cold! I don't like it cold… " You don't have to like it, my dear. Mom's thinking about sunsets at a seaside resort, eating beautiful dishes of ice cream sitting on café terraces, magic dishes with old fashioned and mysterious names: Melba, Copa Cabana… Using this recipe, there's a dish of ice cream with all the frills but without the cold. You make the gateau in a rectangular dish. Thanks to the very dark sugar, it's very sticky. You can also make it with British golden syrup (or corn syrup, from an organic store).

- 7 oz (200 g) dessert chocolate
- 1 1/2 sticks butter
- 1 loosely packed cup brown sugar (very brown and sticky, found in organic stores) or generous
- cup molasses
- 3 eggs
- 2/3 cup all-purpose flour
- Decorations of your choice: chocolate noodles, colored sugar balls, broiled almonds, Chantilly cream (sweetened whipped cream), crystallized cherries, small paper parasols, magic candles…

Preheat the oven to 400 °F (200 °C). Melt the chocolate with the butter over low heat. Add the sugar or molasses, the eggs and the all-purpose flour. Mix vigorously. Bake in the oven for 20 minutes. Beware — the gateau doesn't come away from the mold, or at least not properly: with a tablespoon or an ice cream scoop, hollow out and shape some iced balls or quenelles, and arrange them in small dishes. Decorate them imaginatively.

A bonus: homemade Chantilly cream. It's even better if you add 1 blended banana! This is a recipe pinched from the best waffle stall at the Christmas market in Strasbourg.

Everyone's asleep: the warrior's break

When you suddenly feel a little hungry, pamper yourself. You're dead to the world, as usual! This is the art of warming yourself up, of cheering yourself up in an instant. Take a breather, be selfish—you're allowed a rest. Some of our genuine secrets will perk you up. No cooking, no work, nothing but pleasure before collapsing in the arms of Morpheus or someone else...

Grog
As effective as some remedies sold in the drugstore, for sore throats, colds, or when you're run down!
- Lemon juice
- Clear honey
- Rum
- Warm water

Mix all the ingredients and drink while still very hot.

Pioneers' remedy
A mom never has the right to be ill—it's a well-known fact. For the first signs of common winter ailments, here's a recipe that comes from Vermont and dates from the seventeenth century. It's well known over there—they're all centenarians…
- Cider vinegar
- Tea
- Clear honey

Blend all the ingredients and drink while still very hot.

Strawberries with pepper
This is a real adult thing. Yippee! It does you good.

Chocolate with ginger
Piece of dark chocolate enjoyed with grated fresh ginger.

Slice of raw foie gras with chilli
Use a lot of chilli. It helps you to gather your thoughts—and there aren't too many…

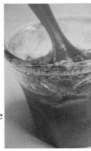

Recommended soundtrack

You have your small iPod, a CD burner... and that's done the trick. These songs, which aren't particularly in tune with the hard job of a mom, are all fantastic. Reconcile yourself to life, to your simplest emotions. Laugh, cry, that does you good. These songs stop you from showing the signs of age, and are a thousand times more effective than chemical treatments or antiaging products sold in the drugstore.

En cloque ("In the family way") — Renaud
Les Roses blanches ("White Roses") — Fréhel
Donnez-lui ("Give him") — Linda Lemay
Oh ! Mammy Blues — Nicoletta
Maman, tu es la plus belle du monde ("Mom, you're the most beautiful woman in the world") — Tino Rossi

Les Yeux de ma mère ("My mom's eyes") — Arno
Le Temps ("Time") — Michel Fugain
Mother's Little Helper — Rolling Stones
Dear Mama — Tupac
"Ah ! vous dirai-je, maman", 12 variations for piano — W. A. Mozart
Médée ("Medea") — Marc Antoine Charpentier
Alceste ("Alcestis") — Christophe Willibald Gluck

And then: have a bath with essential oils (geranium is lovely) and read a good thriller!

Ingredients' index

Apple: Salad of carrot, beet, and apple spaghettis (48), Alsace apple tart (96), Grated apples with rosemary honey and orange (112), Grandma's crystallized apples (114), Fruited bread slices (136).

Apricot: Tiny stew (86).

Avocado: Children's sushis (84).

Banana: Succulent layers (100), Banoffee pie (110), Light cake with banana (126), Fruited bread slices (136).

Beet: Salad of carrot, beet, and apple spaghettis (48).

Broccoli: Pretty broccoli cake (50).

Brown sugar: Sticky chicken (82), Quick flapjacks (132), Iced chocolate gateau balls (152).

Bulgur: Tomatoes stuffed with bulgur wheat risi bisi style (52).

Carrot: Salad of carrot, beet, and apple spaghettis (48), Double treat: wholewheat spaghetti and vegetable spaghettis (60), Shepherd's pie with vegetables (72), Children's sushis (84), Small mouthfuls, balls, and croquettes (142).

Chicken: Browned breaded escalopes (78), Sticky chicken (82), Tiny stew (86).

Chocolate: Smooth chocolate dessert (98), Banoffee pie (110), Chocolate cookies (130), Knights' gateau (146), Iced chocolate gateau balls (152).

Cinnamon: Our potato gratin (58), Tiny stew (86), Mouthwatering crunchy crumble with cream (134), Fruited bread slices (136), Christmas cookies (138), Small mouthfuls, balls, and croquettes (142).

Coconut: Gateau supreme with coconut (116), Coconut mice (140).

Coconut milk: Island fisherman casserole (90).

Fish: Browned breaded escalopes (78), Island fisherman casserole (90).

Ginger: Tiny stew (86), Island fisherman casserole (90), Small mouthfuls, balls, and croquettes (142).

Gorgonzola: Risotto with lemon and Gorgonzola (64).

Ham: Baked ramekins (84), Children's sushis (84).

Honey: Sticky chicken (82), Grated apples with rosemary honey and orange (112), Fruited bread slices (136).

Lamb: Shepherd's pie with vegetables (72), Tiny stew (86).

Lemon: Risotto with lemon and Gorgonzola (64), Island fisherman casserole (90), Soft dessert with lemon (118), Mom's iced strawberry gateau (120), Fruited bread slices (136).

Mango: Island fisherman casserole (90).

Mild mustard: Sticky chicken (82).

Molasses: Quick flapjacks (132), Iced chocolate gateau balls (152).

Nutmeg: Clafoutis with crunchy vegetables (44), Real puree mashed with a fork (54), Grated pancakes (56), Our potato gratin (58).

Oatmeal: Chocolate cookies (130), Quick flapjacks (132).

Orange blossom water: Welcome cake with orange blossom (128), Small mouthfuls, balls, and croquettes (142).

Parmesan: Clafoutis with crunchy vegetables (44), Crumble with polenta and ratatouille confit (46), Double treat: wholewheat spaghetti and vegetable spaghettis (60), Browned breaded escalopes (78).

Pasta: Double treat: wholewheat spaghetti and vegetable spaghettis (60).

Peas: Clafoutis with crunchy vegetables (44), Tomatoes stuffed with bulgur wheat risi bisi style (52).

Pitta bread: Pitta pizza (88).

Polenta: Crumble with polenta and ratatouille confit (46).

Potato: Potato puree mashed with a fork (54), Potato pancakes (56), Our potato gratin (58), Quick French fries (66), Shepherd's pie with vegetables (72), Tiny stew (86).

Quails' eggs: Slice of bread topped with egg (76).

Rice: Risotto with lemon and Gorgonzola (64), Children's sushis (84), Island fisherman casserole (90).

Soft white cheese: Succulent layers (100), Minipancakes with cream cheese, vanilla sugar, and stewed fruits (102), Au pair's cream cheese tart (104), Fruited bread slices (136), Children's buffet (150).

Soy sauce: Sticky chicken (82), Children's sushis (84).

Spinach: Children's sushis (84).

Strawberries: Mom's iced strawberry gateau (120), Fruited bread slices (136).

Sweetened condensed milk: Banoffee pie (110), Gateau supreme with coconut (116), Coconut mice (140), Small mouthfuls, balls, and croquettes (142).

Tomato: Clafoutis with crunchy vegetables (44), Crumble with polenta and ratatouille confit (46), Tomatoes stuffed with bulgur wheat risi bisi style (52), Shepherd's pie with vegetables (72), Mini cordon-bleu parcel (80), Pitta pizza (88), Children's buffet (150).

Turmeric: Island fisherman casserole (90).

Veal: Mini cordon-bleu parcel (80).

Zucchini: Clafoutis with crunchy vegetables (44), Crumble with polenta and ratatouille confit (46), Double treat: wholewheat spaghetti and vegetable spaghettis (60).

The genesis of the book

Friends since the green 1970s era, when their mothers were already buddies, Stéphanie and Aimée are primarily two moms who are very fond of food. Between them, they have 5 children under the age of 5. There's a mixture of aromas in their kitchens: vanilla, chocolate, and dishes simmering with garlic and spices. During their "maternity leave," when they were quite amazed at the crazy direction their lives had taken, they wanted to use their imagination and creativity to foster their passion for good food. They wanted to demonstrate a certain art of living in their homes—full of laughter, friends and clutter—they wanted to talk about the children, food, and life. They needed a book like this one; they looked everywhere for it, but didn't find it. So, they wrote it themselves. But if it weren't their book, they would go out and buy it straightway!

One writes, the other cooks.

Aimée has been an actress, a traveller, a guide for groups of musicians around the world, a consultant, and a scriptwriter, and has run cooking classes with Stéphanie. She pens the texts in this book, having dreamed about, planned, and tested the recipes.

Stéphanie has been a white wine taster, a salesperson at Hermès, and a gallery owner selling Inuit art in Quebec. She set up her own cooking class for children in the Marais district in Paris, and has been running it for two years. She creates the recipes in this book, having dreamed about the texts and laughed when they first appeared...

aclark.langree@wanadoo.fr

stephkaiser@wanadoo.fr

They inspired each other and had a great time.

Thanks to: Louis and Christophe, our husbands, for their patience, their support, and their flair for tasting everything. Thanks to Hugo, Edgar, Basile, Céleste, and Antoine, our children, for their insatiable energy and their love. Thanks to Dahlia and Félix for their sweet smiles and to Isabelle. Not forgetting of course... : our moms, without whom this book would not have been possible; Grandma; Hervé Tardy, our publisher, who had faith in our project; Raphaële, for the way she has captured our recipes; and finally so many people who will recognize themselves across these pages...